Gardening Indoors
with
HOUSE PLANTS

Raymond P. Poincelot

Gardening Indoors
with
HOUSE PLANTS

RODALE PRESS, INC. BOOK DIVISION, Emmaus, Pa. 18049

OB523

First Printing–October, 1974
Second Printing–May, 1975

Photographs by Raymond P. Poincelot, William H. Hylton,
the Rodale Press Photo Lab

Book Design by Repro-Art Service

Illustrations by Erick Ingraham

Plants used in several of the photographs were supplied courtesy of
My Indoor Garden, Allentown, Pa.

Library of Congress Cataloging in Publication Data

Poincelot, Raymond P   1944–
    Gardening indoors with house plants.

    1. House plants. I.   Title.
SB419.P62   635.9'65   74–16238

To my wife, Marian, and my sons, Raymond and Daniel, who are always an inspiration to me. Many thanks to my fellow house plant enthusiasts, Evelyn and Bill, who are always ready to discuss the joys of raising house plants.

Contents

Introduction

I remember my first house plant. It was a small philodendron, which was a free gift from our corner drugstore. Since my wife and I were eager for some greenery during that bleak winter, we eagerly took advantage of this good will gesture. Quickly we carried it home, and to our surprise, this plant thrived in our harsh environment, otherwise known as a desert-dry, steam-heated apartment.

Our success inspired me to greater heights. The next step was to add more house plants that would succeed under our adverse conditions. A visit to the local library yielded a number of books covering house plants. After much searching, I was able to choose some interesting and durable house plants. At that time, I remember thinking a book with an illustrated, alphabetical section with simple, practical commentary on each house plant would be a big help to me. It would have helped me in identifying plants, in knowing cultural requirements and in assessing adaptability and tolerance. Inclusion of practical information necessary for the maintenance of an established house plant collection would certainly have been helpful.

When we left our apartment for a home seven hundred miles away, my house plant collection went with us. It must have been a traumatic trip on the back seat of a car amongst sundry household items, but those tough individuals made it.

Our house had a sun room, which I immediately envisioned as full of house plants. Yes, it even had room for a

garden in the yard. Since I became an organic gardener outdoors, I decided to apply organic growing methods to my
plants indoors. Of course, no books were available on raising
house plants the organic way. I thought back to my first
thoughts on the ideal house plant book; I decided that it
should also explain how to raise house plants by the organic
method.

By now my house plant collection consisted of over a
hundred plants, ranging over all levels of growing conditions.
I had experienced most of the problems common to house
plant growers and found the answers to most of the questions
I had when I first started keeping an indoor garden. Having
gained much confidence with all kinds of house plants, I decided to write this book and share my knowledge with those
who are joining or are already part of the legions of house
plant growers.

I feel certain that you'll find this book quite different
from any other book about house plants. Unlike others, it
embodies the organic concept from natural insect control and
organic fertilizers to extending your food producing season by
growing your fruits and vegetables indoors as house plants. It
answers the questions of beginners and intermediates, and
gives practical information and philosophy on all phases of
raising house plants. The information is applied in the encyclopedic section to aid you in determining at a glance whether
a particular house plant is suitable for your own growing
environment, whether it is a desert-dry, hot apartment, a lush
conservatory, or just an average home. These plants also range
from simple and virtually failproof to extremely challenging.
All in all, there is something for everybody.

This book also goes beyond most books on house plants,
in that it is comprehensive. You need not have several books,
because this book covers such areas as common and specialized house plants; fluorescent gardening; forcing bulbs; growing herbs, vegetables, and fruits indoors as house plants; bottle
gardens, plant maintenance and environment, and house plant
topiary to name just a few.

Most house plants are discussed, including the most re-
cent hybrids. Of course, the growing conditions for each plant
are shown in simple language. Hard-to-find answers to questions like the following will be given: How can I get my

Christmas cactus to bloom without the inconvenience of putting it in a closet at 6:00 P.M.? What plants grow or bloom
better when potbound? What plants thrive on cool temperatures? How do I avoid "greenhouse shock" when I buy a new
plant? What plants put on their best show under fluorescent
lights? What organic fertilizers are best for house plants? In
essence, this book contains everything I had hoped to find in
a book on house plants, but never did.

In closing, I would like to stress one point. Plants are
adaptable to a large degree. Many times I have heard people
say that they did everything wrong, yet the plant survived. My
guidelines are intended as a starting point and once you have
this starting point, it is easy to vary conditions and compare
results.

May your house plants prosper and provide you with
many years of not only a challenging, but a most rewarding
pastime.

Raymond P. Poincelot

Milford, Connecticut, 1974

Section I

The House Plant's Environment

Chapter 1

Of Pots, Soils, Sun, and Air

Pots

House plant fever strikes without warning. Its symptoms are slight, and come to mind only after it is too late. This affliction usually begins innocently enough with the spur-of-the-moment purchase of a plant at the supermarket, five-and-dime, discount store, garden center, or other place. You're attracted by a splash of green or a colorful bloom. You admired a plant in a friend's home; you want to chase away the winter doldrums. And it costs only 89 cents. You water it and it survives. A little while later you buy another plant. Well, you rationalize, the first was lonely. Then one day you happen to pick it up and—horrors!—you find a root dangling from the drainage hole. Now you take the first irreversible step—you march off to purchase some bigger pots. Welcome to the large club of house plant enthusiasts.

The storekeeper says, "What size and what kind do you want?" You know the measurement of your old pot, but you are baffled by the latter. "I thought pots were all made of clay," you reply. "No, we have clay, plastic, styrofoam, and ceramic, which are available in assorted colors and shapes," he replies with a grin. Which one is best?

Each type of pot has both advantages and disadvantages, although some appear to have more of the latter. The traditional pot is made from clay. Some of the advantages of a clay pot are its natural, pleasing appearance and the porosity of the clay, which allows air and water to pass freely through the walls. This air-water diffusion benefits the house plant, because roots require an oxygen-water interaction. While the soil dries out, air enters through the top part of the soil, as well as through the clay side walls. When water slowly passes through the walls, it leaches out some nutrients which, if not removed, could build up to a dangerous level, especially if you overfertilize your plants.

Some disadvantages of clay pots are that they are fragile, they are prone to crusty surface accumulations, and they require much "elbow grease" when they need to be cleaned. Cleaning chores on clay pots will be simple if you don't overwater and don't overfertilize. When you overwater you leach out not only excess nutrients, but also needed ones, resulting in white crusts on the outside of the pot. Overfertilizing obviously aggravates this problem. Furthermore, excess water produces a soggy soil, which causes an imbalance in the oxygen-water uptake at the roots. This is usually followed by total root rot. Once this happens, all that's left to do is to throw that plant away (see Chapters 1 and 3 on watering and drainage).

Always clean a clay pot soon after you remove a plant from it. If you let it dry, it will become more difficult to clean. Use steel wool and cleanser, and rinse well with hot water to remove all the cleanser. Allow it to dry before reusing it. If it is hopelessly encrusted, recycle it by breaking it up with a hammer and use the broken pieces as drainage material.

Plastic pots have several advantages. They are lightweight, resistant to breakage, easy to stack, inexpensive, and simple to clean. Their main disadvantage comes from their lack of porosity. Air and water can enter through the surface of the soil like they do in clay pots; but, unlike clay pots air and water cannot diffuse through the sides. This does not mean that plants grow better in clay pots, because this difference need not be detrimental to plant growth, if slight adjustments are made. The lack of side-wall diffusion simply means less water evaporation and air entry; hence, if the amount of water remains unchanged from that used in a clay pot, the soil becomes soggy and poorly aerated. A possible result is root rot. The obvious solution is to reduce the frequency and amount of water. Personally, I find this reduced frequency of watering works to my advantage because it gives me more time for other things. And this advantage increases with every new plant I get.

Consistent with reducing water is reducing fertilizer.
Since fertilizer can not leach out the sides, an excess can build
in plastic pots quicker than in clay ones and harm a plant. As
a rule of thumb, I find using one half as much water and
fertilizer than I use with clay pots gives comparable results
with plastic pots.

A new line of pots, which I would call both decorative
and functional, has been introduced into the supply line. Some
of these are indeed appealing, especially when you have a
large center-of-display type plant complemented by a decorative pot. However, they can be rather costly if you have a large
number of plants. I prefer to use them in scattered, but strate-
gic spots. In this manner they serve to break the clean, traditional lines of the conventional pots, but they do not become
overpowering.

These types of pots include glazed and unglazed clay, as
well as enameled clay. The glazed and enameled clay are
impermeable to water and air, so they should be handled like
the plastic pots. The unglazed clay, being permeable to air and
water, is treated like the traditional clay pot. These unglazed
pots have etched designs on their sides, unusual shapes such
as globes (great for hanging when filled with trailing plants)
and animals, bizarre colors and even oriental motifs.

Pots in unusual shapes, colors, and sizes are also available
in ceramic, fiberglass, pumice stone, and concrete. For your
large green monsters, you might consider a large fiberglass
pot. Fiberglass is lightweight, but exceedingly strong. The
ceramic and fiberglass pots are more or less treated like plastic
pots, because air and water exchange does not occur through
these materials. The pumice stone and concrete are treated as
if they were clay pots, unless they are glazed or painted.

Finally, there are styrofoam pots. They are lightweight,
inexpensive, porous, and are even insulated, in that the styrofoam prevents rapid changes in the soil temperature. Their
disadvantage is that they dent easily and the white color dirties
quickly. Of course, they do come in a clay color, but I object
to the appearance. My objection is somewhat akin to the feeling a wine lover has about screw caps over corks; I like the clay
color on real clay pots and not on styrofoam.

My own experience with styrofoam pots has not been
favorable. They tip over easily because of their very light

weight. My plants have not progressed as nicely in styrofoam, compared to those growing in clay or plastic pots. Maybe I just have not learned the "tricks" of handling plants in these particular pots; I'll leave them for others to discover.

In this same class, in my opinion, are those rubbery-like plastic pots. They are found often on supermarket house plants and can be easily recognized by their garish colors and flexibility. My plants do not seem to do well in them, so I repot immediately. Perhaps this is traceable to their weak structure. The walls of the pot move easily upon handling and create air gaps between the soil and wall. Root hairs in the vicinity of these gaps become dry, and this can damage the plant.

I use clay and plastic pots, and find good, healthy plants can be grown in both. I like the colors of the various plastic pots scattered amongst the clay ones and find that plastic pots are time-savers, retain moisture well and allow me to cut down on my watering chores. I can even take a weekend sojourn without worrying about watering. I place large plants in plastic pots because they are lighter in weight and are less expensive than comparably-sized clay pots.

However, I put my cacti, succulents, and other infrequently watered plants in clay pots; they just seem to look better with clay and appear to have a slight advantage over similar plants in plastic pots. Since these plants need little water, the plastic pot is not needed.

One important thing I look for in pots is adequate drainage holes. Next time you buy a pot, turn it over. Clay pots usually have one large central hole, and plastic pots have three or four smaller ones. If there are none, you'd do better to look elsewhere for your pots. A lack of drainage holes can only lead to trouble. Sometimes I will buy such a pot if I like its appearance or size, but then I drill five quarter-inch holes in an "X" pattern in the bottom.

Another point I must stress with pots: Wash them with soap and hot water between occupants. I find this simple sanitation procedure aids in preventing plant diseases. It also facilitates the removal of plants from pots. Roots and soil come out neatly in one piece from clean pots, but not from previously dirty ones.

Before leaving the subject of pots, I'd like to briefly mention pot saucers or dishes. Their function is primarily one

of protection because they capture the excess water and prevent water damage to table tops, window sills and such. They
can also be filled with small pebbles, which when moistened,
raise the humidity around the potted plants sitting on these
pebbles. For small pots, *i.e.,* up to four inches in diameter, I
do not purchase saucers because a free substitute is readily
available. Our polyunsaturated margarine comes in gaily
decorated tubs which serve nicely as recycled pot saucers. Of
course, if you have an old set of dishes, the saucers and bowls
(available inexpensively at rummage sales and white elephant
counters) serve equally as well. Aluminum trays and pie plates
are only short-term substitutes; they corrode and leak after a
few months or so. The only pots that I buy regular saucers for
are the very large-sized ones—I haven't found a recyclable
substitute for them.

Soils

Care should be exercised in selecting a soil for your
house plants. After all, you are careful in choosing your own
home to fit your basic needs. It is the same with a plant. Soil
should suit the needs of the particular plants that must inhabit
it over a long period.

Selecting a soil is not all that difficult. Most often it is a
matter of common sense. Plants which come from tropical
forest floors, such as African violets, appreciate a soil rich in
organic matter. Such soil would be similar to the moist humusy
forest soils these plants inhabit in East Africa. Cacti and succulents, coming from arid regions, of course would prefer a
sandy, well drained soil. Those plants which fit neither category, such as begonias, are happy with an all-purpose soil.
(The encyclopedic section in the back indicates the soil type
each plant prefers.)

Basically, I use four soil mixes: an all-purpose mix, two
cacti-succulent mixes, and a humus lover's mix. Each one more
or less is made up of the same ingredients, but in different
proportions.

All contain garden loam, which provides nutrients and a
basic starting structure. I dig the loam from my organic garden
and usually give it a rough screening to remove stones and

other debris. Of course, garden soil varies, but this variance usually is not enough to affect the overall finished mix. If it does, the other materials can be adjusted to compensate for this. I will say more about this later. If garden loam is not available, *i.e.,* you live in an urban apartment building, you can buy packaged soils at reasonable prices. When I lived in an apartment and needed only small amounts I would sneak a little from the flower borders around the apartment building or in a park nearby.

A second ingredient is coarse (not fine) sharp sand. This is not sea sand, which contains harmful salt and is rounded by water action, nor is it water-rounded river sand. Sharp sand is the type used in mortar. It is readily available where building supplies are sold and in some garden centers.

I often picked mine out of the gutter. That's right, the gutter. Rain washes good loam from the land and sweeps it along the gutter. The swift running water carries the loam and finer soil particles along its path, but deposits the heavier sand. I used to find good sand in street gutters, especially near driveways. I'd always wash the road salt out of it once I got it home—salt can be deadly to house plants.

The sharp sand is far superior to rounded sand for drainage purposes, because air and water move more freely through the void space or pores created by the irregular shape of sharp sand. A waterlogged, or poorly drained soil, consequently insufficiently aerated, makes a very unhappy plant whose wet feet turn into a case of root rot. Since this problem is difficult to cure, it is simpler to prepare a properly drained soil.

Another important ingredient is compost or leaf mold. The latter is compost made strictly from leaves. If you live near a woodsy area you can probably collect your leaf mold from the forest floor. If you live in an apartment you might be able to find some under apartment building hedges or obscure corners of the building where leaves collect. Occasionally it's available packaged in garden supply stores. Most people, though, will have to make their own. This is not a problem for most organic gardeners because they make their own compost anyway. Unless you are preparing an acid lover's soil, *i.e.* for azalea, make use of leaf mold prepared from mixed leaves, rather than only oak or pine, which produce an acid leaf mold.

I use mixed compost, which I give a *rough* screening to remove twigs and pebbles. Do not sift it into fine particles, because these larger pieces act to put "give" into the soil, and leave it loose and crumbly.

The addition of compost improves the soil structure and increases the pore volume or air spaces around the particles. Compost also has moisture-holding properties. The sharp sand, because it promotes rapid drainage, counterbalances excessive water-retention. Compost is also a fertilizer, in that it contains various nutrients and trace elements. Some of these are available quickly, while others are gradually released by bacterial and fungal activities. And pieces of compost also supply anchorage for those questing plant roots.

Limestone is contained in some of the soil mixtures. Be sure to purchase the correct form of lime. Avoid quicklime and hydrate of lime; use only ground limestone or dolomitic limestone. Ideally the particle sizes should be a range of sizes so that some limestone is available quickly and the remainder is available over a long period of time. For long-range availability, 100 percent of the limestone should pass through a 10 mesh screen, and about 50 percent should pass through a 100 mesh screen.

Another ingredient in soil mixes is bone meal. Make sure you use the sterilized or steamed form, and not raw bone meal. This is the only organic fertilizer I add to my potting mixes, except, of course, compost which is both a fertilizer and soil conditioner. Between these two, and the nutrients already present in the loam, you will not really need to fertilize your house plants for at least one or two months. Bone meal and compost, being organic fertilizers, will not burn the plant's root system, but will release nutrients and trace elements over a long period of time as they decompose slowly. I will discuss the use of organic fertilizers on established house plants in Chapter 3.

Once you have all your materials, it is advisable to store them, preferably where you will be mixing your potting soils. This way, you'll have the ingredients when you need them and won't have to dash out to the store at the last minute for some sharp sand or dig loam or compost from the garden during winter, when the ground is frozen.

These materials have to be stored somewhere and in

something. Some people have elaborate working benches with storage bins. These are certainly helpful and convenient, but I like to work right where my plants are situated. Bins and work benches would look out of place in my sunroom. So I keep my ingredients underneath a plant table. (If you object to having them in plain view, you can house them in a cabinet and put plants on the top.) When it comes time to repot or propagate, I spread newspapers on or around the table and go to town. When I'm finished I roll up the papers and discard the whole mess.

Containers for your soil ingredients need not be fancy. Any discarded large-size canisters from your kitchen are fine; so are large coffee cans which have snap-on lids. Line metal containers with plastic bags to prevent rusting. The plastic also keeps the material slightly moist, which makes it easier to work. Large-sized tins from soap powder or plastic pails with lids are very useful for holding larger amounts. The latter are available inexpensively in discount stores.

You will need a large scoop to transfer your materials, some type of measuring container, and a mixing container. The items can be bought inexpensively, but you can make all three from plastic half gallon or gallon containers—like those in which bleach is sold.

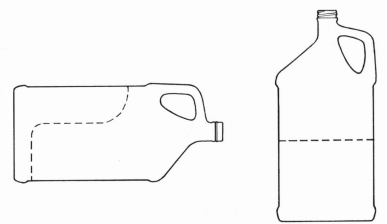

Left: cut on dotted line for scoop with handle; right: use top half for inexpensive funnel and bottom half for measuring container.

Soil mixtures need not be complicated. If you start looking, you can find any number of "recipes." I have four basic mixes which will satisfy almost any house plant. I scoop the required ingredients into my container, and if they are not slightly damp (the dampness of a wrung out sponge), I add a little water. Then I seal the container and shake and rotate it several times to make sure I have a homogeneous mixture.

All-Purpose Potting Mixture
    2 parts garden loam
    1 part compost or leaf mold
    1 part sharp sand
    Add ½ cup of bone meal per peck of above mix or one tablespoon per quart.

Humus Lover's Potting Mixture
    1 part garden loam
    2 parts compost or leaf mold
    1 part sharp sand
    Add ½ cup of bone meal per peck of above mix or one tablespoon per quart.

Cacti and other Succulent Potting Mixtures
    A. Xerophytes (Desert inhabitants)
        1 part garden loam
        1 part compost or leaf mold
        1 part sharp sand
        ½ part crushed clay pot, brick, or small pebbles (approximately pea-sized)
        Add one cup bone meal and one cup ground limestone per bushel or one tablespoon of each to two quarts of soil mixture.

    B. Ephiphytes (Tree crotch dwellers)
        1 part garden loam
        2 parts compost or leaf mold
        1 part sharp sand
        ½ part crushed clay pot, brick, or small pebbles (approximately pea-sized)
        Add one cup bone meal per bushel of soil mix or one tablespoon per two quarts.

These mixtures may be varied to correct for any extreme variances in garden loam. For example, if your garden loam were very sandy, you would slightly reduce the amount of sharp sand. Your state agricultural experiment station or extension service will test your garden loam or soil for you and they will tell you whether it is a sandy loam, clay loam, etc. In some states this service is free and in others there is a nominal charge. However, these recipes will give good results with most garden loams and backyard soils.

A word or two about pH is probably in order at this point. The pH of a soil is a measure of its acidity or alkalinity. On the pH scale, a substance with a pH from 1.0 to 6.9 is acid, one with 7.0 is neutral, and one with a pH of 7.1 to 14.0 is alkaline. You can determine the pH of your soil with pH testers (liquids and papers), which are available in garden supply centers and laboratory supply houses. While these testers are not extremely accurate for determinations of soil pH, they are usually reliable enough for house plant soil mixes. And of course, you may have your soil analyzed for nutrients and pH through your state agricultural experiment station or state agricultural extension service.

Most house plants grow well in soils which are neither very acid nor very alkaline. (Exceptions to this rule will be noted in Section III). In general a pH from 6.0 to 7.0 will suffice for most house plants. To reach that pH range, soil acidity can be decreased by the addition of ground limestone, and to a lesser extent, bone meal; while acidity can be increased by the addition of peat moss, which is acidic.

Soil pH does not have to pose a serious problem for your house plant soil mixes. Usually the loam comes from your garden, and its pH is probably adjusted slightly to an acidic value (pH 6.0 to 6.5), because most garden plants grow satisfactorily at this soil pH. The compost you add has a neutral to slightly alkaline pH, unless it contains many oak leaves or pine needles. As this humus decays in the soil, it produces dilute acids which tend to be neutralized by the added bone meal. In essence, there is a natural "buffering" system, which keeps the pH from becoming too acid or alkaline.

Some house plants, while they grow satisfactorily at a pH of 6.0 to 7.0, do better at lower or higher pH values. For example, many cacti grow in alkaline desert soils. This is why ground limestone is added to the xerophyte cacti and succulent soil mixtures. Other cacti, such as the Christmas cactus, grow in organic matter in tree crotches, which is normally acidic. For that reason, ground limestone is left out of the ephiphyte cacti and succulent soil mixes. Other plants, such as gardenias, also like acid soils. Soil may be kept on the acid side for such plants with a monthly watering of vinegar solution (one half teaspoon per quart of water).

PASTEURIZING YOUR SOIL

Many people assume that home-made potting soil should be sterilized for house plants; they're wrong. You do not want to sterilize the soil and eliminate all living organisms in it. You only want to pasteurize it. Pasteurization is the removal of only the harmful organisms. However, I don't even think that pasteurization of soil is necessary unless there is trouble from nematodes or other soil insects or plant diseases.

If you suspect you have troublesome soil insects or plant pathogens or just want peace of mind, it is a relatively simple matter to pasteurize soil. Place it in a tray and moisten it with water so that it is thoroughly wet for uniform heat conduction. Preheat your oven to the desired temperature. A temperature of 130°F for 25 minutes will kill soil insects, while a temperature of 180°F for 30 minutes will kill plant disease pathogens or microorganisms. Any beneficial fungi or bacteria which are destroyed will be rapidly reintroduced from the air, the debris on the plant roots, and from organic fertilizers. Incidentally, I've never encountered any odor problem while heating the soil as long as it was thoroughly wet.

COMMERCIALLY PREPARED SOIL MIXES

Packaged house plant soils that you can buy in garden centers, hardware stores, flower shops and many department stores, are variable in their composition. I recommend that you try to find a brand prepared with green manure or compost. In my days of apartment living I was fortunate to find a soil mix which stated on the package that it contained organic matter added by the process of green manuring. Some mixes do not state their ingredients. If you are considering buying one of these mixes, examine it closely and see if you can detect any organic matter.

For an all-purpose soil, take three parts of a commercial general-purpose potting soil and add one to one and a half parts sharp sand. This improves the drainage properties of these mixes, which are usually poor because of their powdered texture. For humus lovers take an African violet prepared potting soil and add to it half as much sand. For xerophytes or arid region plants add two parts sharp sand to two parts of commercial all-purpose potting soil. With ephiphytes or p lants dwelling in organic matter collected in tree crotches, add two parts of sharp sand to two parts of African violet prepared soil. Approximately one tablespoon of bone meal per quart of final soil mix should be added to all these mixes.

Sun

Luxuriant house plants are not the result of luck, they're the product of optimal environmental conditions. There are essentially five parameters to be considered: soil, light, temperature, water, and humidity. We have seen already in this chapter how we can regulate soil and will see later how we can control watering, and to a lesser degree, humidity. However, the adjustment of light and temperature in a home is limited; the comfort of our house plants is secondary to our own comfort. For this reason, the simplest way to assure yourself of at least some success with house plants is to allow the prevailing light and temperature conditions in your home to dictate the plants you'll keep there. First I'll be considering light and then temperature. You are wise to remember the interplay of these two factors when considering growing conditions for each house plant. For example, cyclamen will flourish in an east window, *if* the night temperature drops to 50° or 55°F. Both of these requirements eliminate most of our present-day living rooms as a potential site for successful cyclamen growing.

LIGHT

Light is essential to the well-being of plants. It is necessary for the formation of chemical energy in the plant; it also controls some important regulatory and developmental pro-

cesses. House plants let you know when they have too much
or too little light. If they have too much light they may curl
their leaves downward (which they can also do when they
have insufficient humidity) or lose color in their leaves. If they
receive too little light their stems and leaves may become
elongated or they may take on that "reaching upward look"
and lose color in their leaves.

Look around your house or apartment and assess the
availability of light. What you see is what you get, unless you
decide to use fluorescent light units (see next chapter). Generally the light intensity decreases in the following order for the
following window exposures: south, east, west and north, providing there is no large overhang or obstruction of the light
path by an adjacent structure or tree. You must also remember
that the light intensity varies with seasonal changes, being
greater in the summer than the winter. Some house plants may
be perfectly happy at a sunny southern window in the winter,
but unhappy in the summer, unless the light intensity is reduced by a lightweight curtain or the plants are moved some
distance away from the window.

A southern window or sunroom presents the best choice
for growing a wide range of plants. Those that like the sun can
be close to the windows, and those that do not can be placed
farther away, shaded by the sun-lovers. However, do not despair if you don't have a sunroom or large southern exposure.
There are many plants which do quite well in windows receiv-
ing less sun. Some general examples follow:

Those plants that tolerate subdued daylight, *i.e.,* daylight
with no direct sun such as a north window, are Chinese evergreen *(Aglaonema),** cast-iron plant *(Aspidistra),* dumbcane
(Dieffenbachia), Dracaena, rubber plant *(Ficus elastica*
'Decora'), fiddle-leaf fig *(Ficus lyrata),* snake plant *(Sansevieria),* screw pine *(Pandanus veitchi),* kangaroo vine *(Cissus antarctica),* Nephthytis *(Syngonium), Philodendron oxycardium,* and
pothos *(Scindapsus).* This is not to say that the above plants will
be happy in a north window; they will tolerate the low light,
but will perform better in a west or even east window in some
cases.

*For an explanation of plant nomenclature, see the opening of Chap-
ter 11.

Some plants do best with moderate light, such as an east or west window. These include air pine *(Aechmea)*, asparagus fern *(Asparagus plumosus* and *sprengeri)*, begonia *(Begonia semperflorens)*, *Caladium*, umbrella tree *(Schefflera)*, *Peperomia*, piggy-back plant *(Tolmiea menziesii)*, wax plant *(Hoya)*, African violet, *(Saintpaulia ionantha)*, *Dracaena*, *Dieffenbachia*, Moses-in-the-cradle *(Rhoeo spathacea)*, spider plant *(Chlorophytum comosum* 'Vittatum')*, *Philodendron*, pothos *(Scindapsus)*, rubber plant *(Ficus elastica* 'Decora')*, fiddle-leaf fig *(Ficus lyrata)*, snake plant *(Sansevieria)*, prayer plant *(Maranta)*, screw pine *(Pandanus veitchi)*, *Citrus*, Nephthytis *(Syngonium)*, grape ivy *(Cissus rhombifolia)*, aluminum plant *(Pilea cadierei)*, flame violet *(Episcia)*, bromeliads, and ferns.

Other plants are most happy in a sunny southern window. Among these are flowering maple *(Abutilon pictum)*, shrimp plant *(Beloperone guttata)*, crown-of-thorns *(Euphorbia splendens)*, velvet plant *(Gynura aurantiaca)*, geranium *(Pelargonium)*, coleus *(Coleus blumei)*, palms, ivy *(Hedera)*, and succulents.

These categories are not meant to be rigid; they are just suggestive. Your southern window might be shaded by a tree and be equivalent to an east window. You must experiment a bit until you find the best location. Naturally, the above listing does not include all house plants; check Section III for unlisted plants and more detail on those listed above.

Air

TEMPERATURES

Like light, there is little we can do to make major adjustments in temperature just to suit our indoor plants. Fortunately, some plants are very adaptable, and will survive even the inhospitable environments of hot, dry apartments. Furthermore, there are little tricks you can use, besides taking advantage of microclimates in your house, to extend your range of temperatures. The larger the range of temperatures, the greater the number of house plants you can grow successfully.

But just why is a constant temperature bad for house plants? Well, plants, like people, are not all alike. They have their own preferences for different temperatures. They also require a variation in temperature—a drop of a few to several degrees from day to night is good for them.

House plants can be divided basically into three temperature classes: cool lovers, which like daytime temperatures of 55° to 60°F and nighttime temperatures of 40° to 45°F; intermediate temperature lovers, which do best at temperatures of around 70°F during the day and 50° to 55°F at night; and warm temperature lovers, which prefer a daytime high of 80° to 85°F with a night low of 62° to 65°F. These are preferred temperature ranges; smaller variations between night and day temperatures can be tolerated by many plants. However, a nighttime drop in temperature should not be less than 5° to 8°F.

In simple terms, plants at night break down some of the food or carbohydrate, which was produced in the day during the photosynthetic process. This breakdown or respiration provides plants with energy needed for growth. Since part of this breakdown may be wasteful, and as respiration generally increases with increasing temperatures, too high nighttime temperatures may cause decrease in plant growth.

Since each home is different, and what one person wishes to grow, another does not, I can only generalize about temperature regimes and regulation and tell you what I do to adjust temperatures. Firstly, I provide a night drop in temperatures by turning down the thermostat 5° when I retire at night. Not only do my plants love it, but I am convinced that our nightly slumber is better. And turning down the thermostat means, of course cutting down on heating fuel, which means conserving energy and a smaller fuel bill. In the summer, because my windows are open, the temperature drops naturally.

Secondly, I take advantage of the microclimates in my home. You can do the same. Areas near a window may experience a nightly drop in temperature because heat loss is greater through the glass than the insulated wall. This loss becomes localized at the window area, since the movement of air is decreased at night when no one is around to disturb it. A maximum-minimum thermometer placed there and monitored periodically will show the range of temperatures at that site. Pay special attention to that drop on very cold winter nights; you might have to draw that curtain a bit tighter or move the plants away from the window. A southern window will probably be warmer in the day than a northern one, as it receives more sun. Sunporches tend to be cooler at night than other rooms, because of large glass areas favorable for heat loss.

Some rooms in a house can be cooler than others, depending on such factors as the distance the room is from the furnace, the amount of shading by surrounding buildings and trees, the exposure to wind, and the abscence or effectiveness of insulation. Some areas in a home can even be made cooler. For example, a deep bay window can be insulated from the house heat in winter by placing a clear plastic window shade between it and the room. By keeping the shade drawn, the closed-in bay window will be much cooler than the room. You must be careful on very cold nights; you might have to raise this shade "insulator" a bit. (In summer, however, this closed-in area will be warmer than the rest of the house, probably too warm for most plants.)

If you keep your house at 68° to 70°F during the day, drop your temperature about 5° at night, and also take advantage of the various microclimates in your house, you will probably be able to grow most house plants. Experiment with your house plants by moving them to various areas in your house until you find that place where they put on their best performance.

This adaptability and tolerance is really appreciated by those who live in apartments, especially in those apartments where the occupants have no control over the temperatures. Here house plants exhibit the symptoms of too much warmth. Leaves turn yellow or curl and wilt, growth is weak, soft, and spindly, foliage color is light, and buds blast or fall off prematurely. If temperatures become too cold, many leaves may drop off in a short period. However, do not despair if you labor to grow house plants under these conditions. I myself had that problem for three years and found that the following plants would grow even under such conditions: snake plant *(Sansevieria)*, *Philodendron oxycardium*, cast-iron plant *(Aspidistra)*, Chinese evergreen *(Aglaonema)*, *Dracaena*, palms, many cacti and succulents, and other semi-tropical foliage plants (see

Section III for more detailed temperature preferences of many house plants).

HUMIDITY

The amount of moisture in the air is measured in terms of relative humidity. Relative humidity is the actual amount of water vapor in the air at a given temperature, expressed as a percentage of the maximal amount of water vapor that the air could hold at the given temperature.

Fortunately, the range of relative humidity and temperature which is most comfortable to us is suitable for most house plants. A daytime temperature of 68° to 70°F with a 5° to 8° drop at night, and a relative humidity of 50 percent is considered optimal for human health, comfort, and efficiency. A substantial number of house plants grow well under these conditions.

Unfortunately, the relative humidity in many steam and hot-air heated apartments and homes in the winter is closer to 15 to 30 percent. Most air conditioned areas also have a low relative humidity. These low levels, besides being detrimental to the health of many house plants, may affect your respiratory system by drying your mucous membranes. Low relative humidity can give you a raspy throat, dry nose, coughs, and perhaps increase your susceptibility to colds. Low levels of humidity may also cause drying out and possible damage of furniture and house structure, as well as increased heating bills. You use more heating fuel because low humidity makes you feel cool—the increased evaporation of moisture from your skin in dry air causes you to feel chilled. For example, you may feel cold at 76°F and 15 percent relative humidity, but feel warm at 70°F and 50 percent relative humidity. Plants that cannot tolerate low humidity may show browning of leaf tips and edges, yellowing and dropping of lower leaves, and curling or rolling of leaf edges.

You can measure the relative humidity of your rooms with a hygrometer, which should cost at least 10 dollars, if you want a reliable instrument. With levels of relative humidity below 30 percent, you may choose to grow plants tolerant of drier air or to raise the humidity.

Evaporation of water from leaves (or transpiration) is

increased by low humidity and high temperatures, such as one would find in a desert or a hot, dry apartment. Cacti and succulents have succeeded under these conditions, so they are ideal candidates for such apartments. Other possibilities are the very tolerant plants, such as the snake plant *(Sansevieria)*, cast-iron plant *(Aspidistra)*, and *Dracaena.*

Personally I prefer to raise the humidity rather than choose tolerant plants, for my own health, as well as for that of the plant. There are a number of ways of doing this. The most expensive, but most reliable and efficient way is to install a humidifier in your furnace system or use a room humidifier. A simpler, but not as effective way is to suspend containers of water on the back of radiators or from the grate of a hot air duct—just remember to check the pans or dishes frequently and refill them when empty. Of course, you may mist your plants daily, but unless you have a lot of patience, this gets to be a pain in the neck. The window over a kitchen sink or in a bathroom usually has a higher level of humidity than other areas in the house; if possible, place plants that like moist air there.

You can also create a "microclimate" by grouping plants over pebbles which are kept wet. The pots themselves rest on the pebbles, but are not actually in the water. The evaporation of water from the leaves, soil, and pebbles tends to keep the humidity somewhat higher in the immediate vicinity of these grouped plants. For a decorative approach, you might want to try a table fountain with a recirculating pump. Finally, you may obtain very high levels of humidity in an enclosed container, such as a terrarium (see Chaper 5).

POLLUTANTS, CARBON DIOXIDE, AND VENTILATION

Pollution of the air can cause distress to house plants as well as to humans. Gas is probably one of the most common pollutants in the household environment. However, it is manufactured gas, and not natural gas, which causes injury to house plants. Manufactured gas contains ethylene and carbon monoxide: it is these two gases which are chiefly responsible for damage.

Since natural gas is being used in increasing amounts, plant damage due to gas is decreasing. Symptoms of manufac-

tured gas poisoning in plants are rapid yellowing and dropping of most of the foliage. Some flowering plants, such as
African violets, will not bloom, and fruit-bearing plants may
drop their fruit. If you suspect a manufactured gas leak, place
a potted tomato plant in the room. A young tomato plant will
bend its leaves sharply downward within 24 hours if manufactured gas is present. Cooking and heating with this form of gas
does not present a problem. It is only unconsumed, or leaked
manufacturing gas, which harms plants. If you do have trouble, fix any leaks, ignite jets quickly after they are turned on,
make sure the pilot flame does not go out, and keep your flame
adjusted for maximal gas consumption.

Certain plants will tolerate small amounts of manufac-
tured gas. These include pothos *(Scindapsus), Philodendron,
Dracaena,* Nephthytis *(Syngonium),* rubber plant *(Ficus elastica*
'Decora'), amaryllis, cacti, succulents, bromeliads, wandering
Jew *(Tradescantia, Zebrina),* piggy-back plant *(Tolmiea men-
ziesii),* and screw pine *(Pandanus).*

As all of us know, manufactured gas is not the only kind
of pollution. Small amounts of ozone, smog, sulfur dioxide,
hydrogen chloride, ammonia, chlorine, and airborne dirt and
grime are spewed into the air every day and they all damage
house plants. Symptoms of pollutant injury include retarded
growth, leaf drop, and brown or yellow fleck or patches on the
leaves. If you live in areas where these forms of pollution
reach severe levels occasionally, such as with unusual changes
of wind direction or inversion layers, they will probably not
present a serious problem. During these times when levels are
severe, water your plants sparingly, being careful to keep
water off the foliage, and keep the temperature around the
plants lower than normal whenever possible. If you live in an
area which is constantly polluted, you might experiment with
such tough plants as snake plant *(Sansevieria),* cast-iron plant
(Aspidistra), and Philodendron until you find some that tolerate the pollution.

Dirt, dust, and grime, which collect on the leaves of your
house plants, decrease the amount of light received by the
foliage and block the leaf pores (stomata) through which gases
and water vapor diffuse. To eliminate this problem, glossy-
leaved plants should be sponged or sprayed weekly with water
(room temperature), while fuzzy or hairy-leaved plants should

be brushed with a soft camel hair brush. Cleaning leaves is a real chore if you have many house plants; indeed I am lucky if I do it once a month. But even doing it less frequently is beneficial.

VENTILATION

Let us leave the depressing subject of atmospheric pollution and consider a natural component of air, carbon dioxide. Normal levels of atmospheric carbon dioxide are around 300 to 350 parts per million. This is below the level which can be optimal for plant growth. However, there is an increase in the level of carbon dioxide in our homes, caused by our own breathing. These higher levels, sometimes as high as 600 parts per million in the winter with all the windows closed, are beneficial to house plants. However, there can be depletion of carbon dioxide in the immediate vicinity of the leaf surface, when plants use up the carbon dioxide and there is no movement of air to replace it. That is why ventilation is so important for house plants. After all, air circulates around house plants in their natural habitat, and we are trying to recreate the plant's natural environment within the confines of our house.

Ventilation is fairly easy in the summer, spring, and fall, but becomes a problem in our stuffy homes in the winter. One way to keep the air circulating around our plants, if we wish to avoid localized carbon dioxide depletion, is to put them where there is movement of people. If you have house plants in untraveled areas, no one will be able to enjoy them anyway. Sometime during the day, try to open a window slightly in another room, even if it is only for a half hour. Never subject a plant to a direct draft of cold air. If you must open a window in your plant room, use a window ventilator to prevent a draft.

Good ventilation can also prevent plant disease. If there is no air circulation around the leaves of the plant, there is not only a depletion of carbon dioxide, but a localized increase in water vapor transpired by the plant. This may condense on the leaves, providing ideal conditions for the germination of spores from plant pathogens (disease-producing microorganisms).

As I have pointed out already, heating and air condition-
ing do not pose a problem for house plants, as long as you
maintain temperature and relative humidity in the ranges for
human comfort and efficiency. With both heating and cooling,
it is important to avoid a direct draft on your plants. Drafts can
dry or dessicate your plant, causing wilting, yellowing, or
falling of leaves.

Chapter 2

Bringing the Sun Indoors

At one time the location of indoor plants was limited by the availability of natural light. Sun cannot penetrate solid walls to reach those dark nooks and alcoves; its effectiveness is hindered by cloudy and rainy weather; and it cannot be turned on with the flick of a switch. This all changed with the invention of artificial light and its use in indoor gardens. People are not the masters of the sun, but they are the masters of their fluorescent light units, as long as they pay the electric bills.

The use of fluorescent lamps to grow house plants has increased rapidly in the last several years. These lamps may completely replace the sun as a light source, converting dark areas, such as basements, into lush indoor gardens. They can also supplement weak natural light, as in a north or heavily shaded window or on a dreary winter day. Cuttings seem to root much quicker and seedlings seem to develop much better under artificial rather than natural light. Terrariums and aquariums are ideal subjects for artificial lighting. Displays of plants lit with artificial light can be focal points in your interior decoration plans.

By growing plants with only artificial light, you can regulate their day length and bring plants into bloom at times other than their normal outdoor blooming time. For example, florists can bring poinsettias into bloom for Christmas by giving them 60 days of short day length (less than 12 hours of artificial light.).

In effect, these artificial light sources do not completely duplicate the physical parameters of sunlight. However, they

23

do reproduce the growth responses brought about with sunlight by providing the intensities and light wavelengths most
effective for the various growth responses.

Light does effect several processes in the plant. Among
these are photoperiodism, phototropism, photonasty, and
photosynthesis. The response of vegetative growth and reproductive activities in plants to the duration of light and dark
periods is called photoperiodism. I will discuss photoperiodism further in Chapter 6, because it plays a key role in the
seasonal bloom of such plants as Christmas cactus. Phototropism is a growth movement in response to one-sided illumination. An example of phototropism is the leaning of sunflowers
toward the sun. Photonasty is a light-stimulated movement of
stems or leaves that, unlike phototropism, has no relation to
the direction from which the light arrived. An example of
photonasty is the "sleep" movements of beans: during the day
the first pair of leaves above the cotyledons are horizontal and
at night they are folded downward alongside the stems. Finally, photosynthesis is the process by which plants convert
carbon dioxide and water in the presence of light and chlorophyll into carbohydrates and oxygen. Of all the light responses
described here and other light processes not mentioned, the
process of photosynthesis is really the determining factor in
choosing effective artificial light sources for successful house
plant growing.

*Some of the author's house plants under artificial lights. The fluorescent lamp fixture
shown here is the industrial type—it is free-hanging and has a built-in reflector. Notice
the timer that automatically turns the lamp on and off.*

Scientists have shown that not all of the light reaching plants is used in the photosynthetic process. Only certain wavelengths in white light (*i.e.,* colors) are "trapped" or absorbed by chlorophyll. The various wavelengths or colors composing white light are readily seen when light passes through a prism (they may also be seen in a rainbow). The colors include violet, indigo, blue, green, yellow, orange, and red. Chlorophyll absorbs essentially the wavelengths comprising the blue and red range and transmits or reflects the green wavelengths. The green color of plants is derived from the transmission of these green wavelengths.

Accordingly, the ideal lamps should be richest in the blue and red areas of the spectrum. Fluorescent lamps come much closer than incandescent lamps to meeting this criterion. Fluorescent lamps also have additional advantages. They are approximately three times more effective than incandescent lamps in converting electrical energy into light and therefore produce less waste heat, they have a lifetime which is generally 15 times as great as the incandescent bulb, and their light distribution is more linear.

However, some fluorescent lamps are much more effective for growing plants than others. Cool white fluorescent lamps can be used for plant growth, but they were really designed for visual purposes. Their wavelength output will not produce maximal plant growth responses because the color output in decreasing order is yellow-green, blue, and red. For this reason they are often supplemented with incandescent bulbs which are rich in the red region. Rather than describing the merits of each lamp in words, it is probably simpler to do it in table form. See Table I. I should like to point out that besides the red region, there is also a far red section in the spectrum. Most foliage house plants principally require the red and blue portions, but vegetables and many flowering plants also require a far red source in addition to the blue and red.

At first glance Table I may appear somewhat confusing, but a little thought shows it to be an excellent guide when choosing lamps for your gardening with artificial light. For example, if you wish only to grow foliage plants with these light sources, most scientific studies indicate that the energy levels should decrease in the following order: red, blue, and yellow-green. However, if you wish to grow vegetables and many flowering plants under lights, the studies show that the energy levels should decrease as follows: red, far-red, blue, and yellow-green.

From my own endeavors with fluorescent lights and from the studies of others, I have reached my own conclusions, which may guide you in your selection of lamps. For growing foliage plants, vegetables, and flowering plants I have found that the Gro-Lux wide spectrum fluorescent lamp is quite satisfactory. For raising seedlings, propagating cuttings, and forcing bulbs; I would choose a combination of standard Gro-Lux and the wide spectrum Gro-Lux. I think it has a slight edge over wide spectrum Gro-Lux alone.

This is not to say that other combinations will not give you good results. For example, before the wide spectrum Gro-Lux appeared, the standard Gro-Lux seemed to have a slight edge over the combination of daylight/natural, a larger

TABLE I.   Relative Energy Output of Various Fluorescent and Incandescent Lamps in Certain Spectral Regions

Lamp	Blue	Yellow-Green	Red	Far Red
Incandescent	L	H	VH	M
Cool White	H	VH	L	VL
Daylight	VH	VH	VL	VL
Warm White	M	VH	M	VL
Natural White	L	VH	VH	VL
Gro-Lux (Sylvania)	VH	L	H	VL
Plant-Light (General Electric)	VH	L	H	VL
Plant-Gro (Westinghouse)	VH	L	H	VL
Wide Spectrum Gro-Lux (Sylvania)	M	H	H	L
Cool White/Incandescent*	M	VH	H	L
Daylight/Natural**	M	VH	M	VL
Daylight/Warm White**	H	VH	L	VL
Gro-Lux/Wide Spectrum Gro-Lux**	H	M	H	L

Abbreviations: Very Low (VL), Low (L), Medium (M), High (H), and Very High (VH).
*100 watts/30 watts
**1:1 ratio

edge over daylight/warm white, and the largest edge over cool white alone. However, none of these were extremely effective with vegetables or many flowering plants. Results were greatly improved when either cool white or Gro-Lux (standard) were supplemented with incandescent light. This improvement resulted from the far red spectral contribution from the incandescent bulb. From these results, the wide spectrum Gro-Lux was developed. It had the advantages of the combined standard Gro-Lux/incandescent or cool white/incandescent, because in addition to spectral emissions in the blue and red areas, it also had some emission in the far red region.

Some of the advantages of the wide spectrum Gro-Lux are that it can be used for foliage plants, vegetables, and flowering plants, being essentially two bulbs in one (no more incandescent sockets and heat problems). It costs somewhat more than cool white, but much less than standard Gro-Lux (the phosphor used in the manufacturing of the wide spectrum form is much less expensive than the one in the standard form), and the "weird" purple glow of the standard form is replaced by a restful pale pink (some people like the purple glow; I do not).

Although I have only mentioned Gro-Lux, the other plant lamps, Plant-Gro and Plant-Light, have similar spectral emissions. I have not personally used them, but it appears they are very similar in performance to the standard Gro-Lux. I am not aware of any variations of these that are similar to the wide spectrum Gro-Lux.

Invariably people with fluorescent light units want to measure the intensity of their lamps. My own opinion is: do not bother yourself with this problem; measure your lamp output indirectly from the growth responses of your plants. A good light meter is expensive, and it only measures light in terms of foot-candles. But, as I explained above, you should measure the energy emission in the blue, red and far red spectral regions if you want a true measure of a bulb's effectiveness for plant growth. Indeed, this is the method that scientists use. However, meters that measure the color regions are not readily available. If you think the investment would be worth it, there is a relatively low cost meter that measures energy directly in these spectral bands. (See Appendix.)

I don't bother with meters—I prefer to indirectly judge the effectiveness of the lamps at various heights from the observed growth responses. Three different plants act as my "living indicators" of the light output. They are the velvet plant *(Gynura aurantiaca)*, which is a high output indicator; the aluminum plant *(Pilea cadierei)*, which is a medium output indicator; and *Philodendron oxycardium ("cordatum")*, which is a low output indicator.

Briefly, here's how to use my system. First, you have to realize that the brightest part of the fluorescent tube is at the center and the dimmest part is at the ends. As a rough guide, a distance less than 8 inches from the center of a wide spectrum Gro-Lux lamp (I use two 40-watt sizes per fixture) to plant foliage would give what I call high light intensity. Eight to 12 inches would be medium and 12 to 18 inches would be low light intensity. These are only approximate distances (any available natural light would change the distance) and would vary for other lamps; they are merely meant as guidelines. Now you take a reading with your "living indicators." Put your plants under the fluorescent tubes and observe them for a month. If you give them proper cultural care, indicator plants will respond as follows: The velvet plant will be colored a rich royal purple under high intensities; it will be green under lesser intensities. The aluminum plant will be a rich green with outstanding silver markings under medium intensities and the *Philodendron oxycardium* will be green and healthy if grown under low intensities. There is one other factor to keep in mind. If a plant receives too much light, its leaves may curl downward or hug the sides of the pot (as if it were retreating from the light) and the green color may be bleached out. On the other hand, insufficient light will cause an elongated appearance, a "reaching upward" look, and a pale green leaf. This is true with natural or artificial light. Of course you may put one or more types under your lamps, because there is a decrease in light intensity from the center of the tube to the end.

In Table II, I have listed some house plants which can be grown or supplemented with artificial light. The list is not meant to be inclusive; it serves merely as a guide. If a plant is not on the list, try it anyway! Remember, the growth of

Low (12 to 18 inches)
Cast-iron plant (*Aspidistra elatior* ["*lurida*"])
Chinese evergreen (*Aglaonema modestum*)
Ferns
Nephthytis (*Syngonium*)
Medium (8 to 12 inches)
African violets (*Saintpaulia*)
Aluminum plant (*Pilea cadierei*)
Begonia metallica
Begonia rex
Bromeliads
Bulbs (daffodils, hyacinth, tulip, etc.)
Dracaena
Dumb cane (*Dieffenbachia*)
Ficus macrophylla
Grape ivy (*Cissus* ["*Vitis*"] *rhombifolia*)
Norfolk Island pine (*Araucaria excelsa*)
High (below 8 inches)
Asparagus fern (*Asparagus plumosus*)
Begonia (other than *B. metallica* and *B. rex*)
Cacti
Citrus
Coleus blumei:
Croton (*Codiaeum variegatum*)
Fiddle leaf fig (*Ficus lyrata* ["*pandurata*"])
Flowering annuals
Geraniums (*Pelargonium*)
Gesneriads (other than *Saintpaulia*)
Ivy (*Hedera*)
Kalanchoe

Screw pine (*Pandanus vietchi*)
Snakeplant (*Sansevieria*)
Philodendron oxycardium ("*cordatum*")

Orchids (shade-loving types: *Cypripedium, Phalaenopsis*)
Palms
Peperomia
Philodendron (other than *P. oxycardium*)
Pothos (*Scindapsus*)
Prayer plant (*Maranta leuconeura kerchoveana*)
Rubber plant (*Ficus elastica* 'Decora')
Spider plant (*Chlorophytum comosum* 'Vittatum')
Umbrella tree (*Schefflera*)
Wandering Jew (*Tradescantia, Zebrina*)

Medicine plant (*Aloe vera*)
Moses-in-the-cradle (*Rhoeo spathacea*)
Orchids (sun-loving types: *Cattleya, Cymbidium, Dendrobium, Epidendrum, Oncidium,* and *Vanda*)
Patience Plant (*Impatiens*)
Shrimp plant (*Beloperone*)
Succulents
Tree ivy (*Fatshedera*)
Vegetables
Velvet plant (*Gynura aurantiaca*)
Wax plant (*Hoya carnosa*)
Zebra plant (*Aphelandra squarrosa*)

plants under lamps is a substitute for growth with natural light, but there is no substitute for the other environmental needs of the plants, like temperature, water, and humidity. (See Section III for information about the cultural requirements of various plants.)

One last point—the "living indicators" picked are only three possible choices. If you do not have those plants, pick substitutes from their respective groups.

Fixtures and Bulbs

Now we are ready to set up the mechanical end of our lights and fixtures. First, there are basically two types of fluorescent lamp fixtures. They are the industrial and strip (also called channel) fixtures. The industrial type has a built-in reflector, whereas the strip type does not. Usually the industrial type is hung in the open, where there is no reflective source other than the built-in reflector. It is usually raised and lowered with adjustable chains that hook into the fixture. The strip type is used under shelves or cabinets, and the supporting background is painted with flat white paint and acts as a reflector. Flat white, even though it may not appear so to your eye, reflects more light than glossy white. Unfortunately, the industrial fixture is normally available with glossy white baked enamel. For maximal light reflection, this should be removed with paint remover and repainted with flat white. The strip fixture is usually slightly less expensive than the industrial kind. Both are available in one, two, three, or four tube models which accommodate 20-watt (24 inch), 40-watt (48 inch), or 72, 73, 74, 75-watt (96 inch) lamps. It is my own experience that it is best to buy either the 40-watt or 72-watt size, because the bulbs are more readily available in these sizes. One 40-watt size tube lights a growing area of approximately 48 inches by 6 inches and one 72-watt size serves an area 96 inches by 6 inches. Of course, two bulbs double the area, and so on.

There are three types of bulbs which are available. They are the preheat lamp, the rapid start lamp, and the slimline instant start lamp. The preheat lamp is available in the following wattages: 15, 20, 30, and 40. This lamp requires a starter and is the most economical, because it requires a low cost ballast, lamps last longer (lower circuit voltage can be used with a starter), and light output is high. They also start better under high humidity conditions.

The rapid start lamp requires no starter, turns on in one or two seconds, and operates with a smaller, quieter ballast. They are available in 30- and 40-watt sizes. Of course, the rapid start lamps may be used in either a preheat or rapid start fixture. They burn out quicker and are sometimes troublesome in starting in high humidity.

The slimline instant start lamp also has no starter and turns on rapidly. These lamps have a single pin on each end (the preheat and rapid start have two pins on each end), and they are much easier to install in their single hole push-pull socket, as opposed to the double pin, align, twist-turn types. Slimline lamps can only be used in a slimline instant start fixture, which has a higher voltage ballast than the other types. They are available in most wattages.

Which lamp, which fixture, what size, *etc.* should I use? Well, I am not sure I can give you the complete answer, but maybe I can help you to make up your own mind. The type of fixture is a matter of choice governed by the area in which it is to be used. I have both the industrial and strip types, although most of them are the industrial kind. If you are using the four-foot size fixture (anything less in my opinion is inefficient for growing plants), get the fixture with the starter designed for preheat lamps because of the already described economy and good performance in high humidity. The slimline fixture is better, I feel, but I found better bargains with the preheat type when I needed my fixtures.

As far as I know, the eight-foot fixture is only available in the slimline instant start fixtures. I have both the four-and eight-foot length fixtures, since each one has its own merits. The eight-foot fixture is very long, and many areas will not accommodate this awkward size. By adjusting two four-foot fixtures to two different heights, you can have two separate light intensities in the same area. Obviously, you can't do this with an eight-foot fixture. However, the eight-foot fixture is more efficient. Because it has only two ends and the two shorter tubes together have four ends, the decrease in light output at the ends would be less. And the older the tubes are, the greater this difference in efficiency, since this decrease in light output increases with age due to blackening.

As for what kinds of tubes to use, I have already pointed out that I favor the Gro-Lux (standard and wide spectrum), which are available in preheat, rapid start, and instant start forms in most wattages.

Life Expectancies of Bulbs

Manufacturers of fluorescent lamps give suggested life expectancies based on the assumption that a bulb will be lit for three hours per start. Since the process of starting contributes greatly to the wear and tear of a fluorescent tube, the longer you burn it per start, the higher the life span. Roughly, the life span of a 40-watt preheat bulb burned three hours per day is 16,000 hours, or 24,000 hours if burned 12 hours per day, and 27,000 hours if burned 18 hours per day. Rapid start lamps would have a somewhat shorter life span. Because manufacturers are constantly improving the life span of fluorescent bulbs, it would be best to write to the manufacturer of your bulb and request information on its service period.

Most under-light gardeners (including myself) suggest that you replace a bulb when it reaches 75 percent of its rated service life. They also suggest that you stagger replacement by replacing one bulb per week. This is to prevent a "light shock" to your plants, which become accustomed to the gradual dimming of light. As an example, I burn some of my Gro-Lux lamps (40-watt) for 14 hours per day and replace them after a period of two to two and one-half years. I replace them sooner if I detect heavy blackening at the tube ends, which means the lamp is near its end. To aid my memory, I mark the starting date on the glass near the end with magic marker.

After a new fluorescent lamp is installed, you may observe a snake-like flickering of the light. This will go away when the new lamp is seasoned. Grayish (not black) deposits from mercury may also be observed at the ends of new bulbs. These too will disappear with time. Occasionally, after the lamp has gotten over its seasoning, a gray band will be observed about two inches from one or both ends of the tube. Such bands have no effect on the quality of light output. However, if heavy blackening develops at the ends of the tube, sometimes associated with the light flashing on and off, you can be relatively sure the lamp is near the end of its service. If your lamps blacken prematurely and consistently, your equipment—and not the fluorescent tubes—is probably at fault. Defective starters, extremes in temperature, bad ballasts, fluctuations in the line voltage, and defective wiring could be responsible for premature aging of fluorescent tubes.

Lamps and fixtures should be cleaned at least once a month to remove dust and grime, since both of these interfere with the light emitted. However, when you wipe lamps you not only remove dirt, you also remove a silicone coating which was applied by the manufacturer, to make lamps start readily under high humidity and other extreme conditions. This coating can be replaced readily by spraying a cloth with a silicone lubricant (found at hardware, automotive, and discount stores) and giving the glass tube a wipe.

Ballasts

Ballasts maintain the current in your lamps at the proper operating level. Without them, the current would run unchecked and could destroy the lamp. Usually the ballast comes as part of the lamp fixture. However, if you are going to have an extensive set-up with numerous lamps, you can buy the ballasts separately and install them at a location other than near your plants and lamps. This is advisable, since the ballasts give off most of the heat emitted by a fluorescent lamp unit. Normally, with single or small groupings of unenclosed lamps, this heat does not present a problem, because the fixture is designed to radiate the heat upward. But if the lamps are enclosed in a case or there are a large number of them, it does present a problem. Installation of ballasts separate from the lamps should be done by an experienced electrician.

Ballasts come in two forms: the high-power factor ballast and the low-power factor ballast. The high-power factor ballast utilizes less electricity than the low-power factor ballast to produce the same amount of light. Although the high-power

factor ballast costs more initially, in the long-run, the savings
in electrical costs makes it more economical than the lower-
power type. Some ballasts are noisy; they have a disturbing
humming sound. More expensive ballasts, of course, are less
noisy. If you can afford it, it is best to purchase fixtures with
high-power factor ballasts. If the ballast that comes with your
fixture burns out (smoking and making an awful smell), you
can replace it, preferably with a high-power factor ballast.
Ballasts in general can last for up to 10 or 12 years.

Power Switches and Time Controls

Every fluorescent lamp should have an on-off switch.
You may install an "in line" switch or a fixture-mounted
switch. I prefer the latter, whether it be a toggle, push button,
or pull chain switch. Knockout plugs are usually provided in
the fixture for fairly simple installation. The purpose of such
a switch is obvious: When you are changing a bulb, or when
you are having trouble with a particular lamp, you can turn off
one lamp that is hooked up to a time switch set-up without
turning off all the other lamps controlled by the time control.

I use a time control switch for all my lamps for two
reasons. First, I never have to forget to turn them on or off,
and secondly, it gives my house a lived-in look when I'm away.
When you purchase such a time control switch, make sure that
it can handle at least 1500 watts, that it is approved by Under-
writers Laboratory, and that it can be adjusted over a 24-hour
span.

Arranging Your Indoor Fluorescent Light Garden

Probably, the simplest place for an indoor garden is a
table of some convenient size whose surface is protected by
plastic sheeting. Clear, colored, or patterned plastic can be
purchased inexpensively; it comes in rolls and is commonly
used for upholstery. One or more industrial fixture can be
suspended over it with adjustable chains. Then plants can be

placed on the table at various heights, or stagings, by putting them directly on the table top, or on pots, inverted glasses, *etc.*, to create the proper light conditions for each. Plants should be situated to conceal the "height adjusters."

You can create a larger indoor garden by setting up a three-tiered bench with strip fixtures on the undersides of the top and middle shelves, and an industrial fixture suspended over the top. The shelf tops of such benches are usually protected with plastic and the undersides painted flat white. Because the shelves usually have sides, you can line the bottom of each with pea gravel or vermiculite. Keep the vermiculite or gravel moist to increase the humidity around your plants. To discourage root rot and prevent spread of disease, I recommend that you place your pots on rust-proof racks, and not directly in the moist material.

If you plan to build your own plant tables or tiered benches, make them strong. Wet gravel or vermiculite, pots, soil, and large numbers of plants, not to mention fluorescent fixtures, can be very heavy. Choose materials that are waterproof. High humidity and leaking water can rot wood and rust metal if these materials are not properly protected. (See Appendix for sources of indoor gardening equipment.)

In closing, I would like to make the following precautions. If you know very little about electricity and wiring, buy prewired fixtures or have an electrician do it. Furthermore, if you plan on several or more fixtures, determine the total wattage so that you will not overload your household electrical circuits. A rough rule of thumb is that ballasts use 10 watts for every 40 watts of light. Therefore, a fixture with two 40-watt bulbs and the ballast would consume 100 watts.

Section II

New Plants Move in to Stay

Chapter 3

Keeping That Vibrant Green
with Water and Organic Fertilizers

New Arrivals

If you are an enthusiastic house plant grower, there will probably be frequent new arrivals at your home. These house plants may come from friends, a greenhouse, a supermarket, or other places, but whatever their origin, they should all be treated alike. That is, you should put them through an inspection and quarantine (after your friend leaves), just like they were astronauts returning to earth. The reason is very simple: to prevent the introduction of insects and diseases into your established plant habitat.

Pick up your new arrival and inspect the bottom drainage hole. Are roots protruding from it? Place your hand over the surface of the soil, spread your fingers around the plant stem, and turn the pot upside down. Tap the pot gently until the ball of soil and the pot separate. Are roots all entwined around the surface of the ball of soil or is it a solid mass of roots? If the answer is yes to either of these questions, the plant needs repotting. Even when I find myself answering with a no, I still repot the plant. At least I know what is in my own soil mixtures (see Chapter 1 for soil mixtures and Chapter 5 for repotting). Then I proceed to carefully wash the plant with a forceful spray (not too forceful for fear of plant damage) of room temperature water to dislodge any insects, and to remove any dust or grime. Then I let the plant dry in a room free of drafts and out of the sun. When dry I give it a thorough examination for insects and disease (see Chapter 5 for insect and disease problems). I keep this new arrival under observation for two weeks in a separate room, being careful not to touch it and then touch my other plants because some diseases can be transmitted by contact. If at the end of two weeks it is healthy and free of insects, I bring it into my plant habitat.

Sometimes a new arrival appears healthy, but soon undergoes a dramatic change. The leaves droop, wilt, yellow, or dry, and subsequently fall off. I call this the "greenhouse shock syndrome." It usually occurs during the cold months when your home is heated and your relative humidity is low. The situation can be remedied quite simply: Do not buy a house plant from the greenhouse during the winter. That is easier said than done. When it is a dreary winter day and you are in a commercial greenhouse, you may find it hard to resist a new addition. If you buy it, and you know your relative humidity is below 40 percent, you can beat the problem. Enclose your plant in a plastic bag and open it gradually over a two week span. Your plant slowly acclimates itself to the different humidity level, avoiding a traumatic, and often fatal, shock. Of course, these new arrivals need watering, which brings us to the next subject.

Watering

Undoubtedly, the hardest thing to tell a new house plant grower is how much water to give a plant. There is no simple rule. Experience is probably the best teacher. However, there are some helpful hints which will start you off on the right foot.

I do not use city water directly from the tap because it contains chlorine and is not always at room temperature. Chlorine can be removed by placing the water in uncapped containers (like the gallon plastic jugs that apple cider and milk come in), and allowing them to stand for 24 hours. After this length of time, the chlorine will have diffused into the air and the water will be at room temperature. Well water would only need to stand until it reaches room temperature. I keep several jugs on hand and always refill each one as I empty it. The jugs are only for storage; I water my plants with a long-neck plastic watering can. Such cans are lightweight, do not rust, and easily allow me to water inaccessible areas without wetting leaves and table tops.

If you soften your water with ion exchangers (for example, Zeolite), a word of caution is in order. Do not water your plants with water that has gone through the ion exchange resin, because this type of softened water could be harmful to your plants.

In very broad terms, the watering requirements of houseplants can be lumped into three categories: Those that like dry periods between watering, such as cacti; those that like to be moderately moist, but neither soggy nor dry, like African violet; and those that like constant wetness and will not tolerate drying out, such as American maidenhair fern.

Unfortunately, such categorization is an oversimplification because other factors affect watering needs. For example, plants in glazed pots, plastic pots, and ceramic pots need about one-half the water a plant in a clay pot would need (see Chapter 1). This is because the pot walls in non-clay pots are not porous and allow evaporation of water only from the surface soil. The relative humidity influences the frequency of watering. On damp or rainy days, water does not evaporate as readily from the pot or transpire as quickly from the plant; however, plants in a steam-heated apartment might require watering daily. Some plants also undergo a rest or dormant period, at which time their watering must be reduced. A pruned plant or a sick plant will need less water than an unpruned or healthy one. An older root-bound plant needs more water than its younger counterpart. All these factors combine to interfere with a fixed, rigid schedule of watering. Plants must be watered according to their individual needs.

Try to familiarize yourself with each plant. Look up its cultural requirements in Section III, and pay special attention to its water requirement. No matter how often it needs to be watered, one thing will hold true for every plant: When you water it, water it thoroughly. If you use a watering can, which I always do, add water to the pot until it comes out the drainage hole. If you have pebbles in the saucer, leave enough water to keep the pebbles moist. If not, pour off all the water —do not let any set in the bottom of an empty saucer. Leaving water deep enough in a saucer so that capillary action can draw excess water into the potting soil could lead to root rot. If you practice bottom watering, pour off the excess from the saucer when the top soil becomes wet.

I personally prefer a thorough top watering over bottom watering because it flushes out the soil, removing surplus nutrients and preventing a build-up of soluble salts, which in excess can be harmful to the plant. Soluble salts can accumulate even with organic fertilizers (see the discussion of fertilizers, later in this chapter). And in their natural habitat, plants are top-watered by rain. Watering thoroughly has a purpose: It encourages uniform root distribution. Watering just enough to wet the surface encourages roots to form there only. When the soil surface dries out, so do these roots. The plant must then grow new ones at the expense of foliage and flowers.

While all the plants should get a thorough drenching each time they are watered, the frequency of watering is influenced by environmental factors and varies with each plant.

Plants such as cacti and other succulents enjoy a dry period between waterings. This period might vary from a week to a month, depending on previously mentioned factors. More plants than not need water when the top one-half inch of soil feels dry to the touch. After a while, you will develop a feel for each plant's water needs.

Overwatering is probably more detrimental to a plant's health than underwatering. The root system of a plant takes in water, nutrients, and oxygen. When you water a plant, the water displaces air in the void volume or spaces between soil particles. This exchange is often observed as air bubbles rising from the soil's surface through the standing water. As the soil drys, air again re-enters these spaces between soil particles. This supplies oxygen for root respiration and also stimulates the growth of roots in search of moisture in the drying soil. However, overwatering prevents the re-entry of air. The fine root hairs develop root rot and stop their active growth. Leaves begin to yellow and fall off and stems get rotted, mushy, and dark in color. Immediate reduction of watering and drying periods between each watering might revive a plant with such symptoms of advanced root rot. If, on the other hand, a plant does not get enough water, it expresses its displeasure by leaf and stem wilting. Prompt watering usually revives it. Lack of water is not fatal, unless it occurs often, or you let a plant remain wilted for too long a time.

When is the best time for watering your plants? The morning is usually considered to be better than the evening.

However, not being independently wealthy, I do have to go
to work. Therefore I water my plants in the evening, taking
care not to splash water on the leaves. My plants have never
seemed to complain about not being watered earlier in the day.

Organic Fertilizers

The growth responses of house plants appear to be better
with constant, weak applications of nutrients as opposed to
strong applications at regulated intervals. Strong doses of water soluble nutrients at spaced intervals can damage tender
root hairs and cause too rapid a growth of plant tissue. More-
over, powerful nutrients can be leached out of the soil by
subsequent waterings before they are fully utilized, possibly
leading to a period of nutrient deficiency prior to the next
application of fertilizer. This feast-or-famine type of diet is not
good for plants.

The best way to assure yourself that your plants are getting a steady, moderate diet is to use organic fertilizers. They
will not burn the delicate root hairs, and the gradual release
of their nutrients assures a constant supply. Furthermore, no
damage is done if you forget an application or two, or if you
mistakenly add too much. You probably have heard the old
phrase which says that imitation is the sincerest form of flat-
tery. Well, chemical fertilizers now come in pelleted plastic
forms which yield up their nutrients gradually over a period
of time. It would appear that the chemical companies have
discovered something that the users of organic house plant
fertilizers have known for many years: a slow release of nutrients is best for plants. Another advantage of organic fertilizers
is that they can be applied to dry soil without fear of burning
house plant roots. Many chemical fertilizers must be added to
wet soil.

Organic fertilizers can supply nitrogen, phosphorus,
potassium, and trace elements. All of these are essential for
healthy plants, be they indoor or outdoor types.

Nitrogen is a positive factor in dark green leaf color and
strong vegetative growth. It is also necessary for protein syn-
thesis in the plant. If too much nitrogen is present, lush but
weak foliage is produced at the expense of blossoms. A lack

of nitrogen produces stunted plants and yellowing of bottom foliage, which proceeds to work its way upward. Unlike the yellowing caused by a water shortage, which strikes at the bottom and top foliage at the same time, yellowing due to an excess of nitrogen starts on the leaf edges and works back to the petiole, or stem. It is also different from yellowing due to iron deficiency; in such cases, the veins tend to stay green while the rest of the leaf yellows. Nitrogen is usually taken up from the soil at a greater rate than the other nutrients. It is also prone to leaching when plants are watered. However, as I explain below, you won't have this leaching problem if you use organic fertilizers.

Phosphorus promotes good blooming and the formation of strong root systems in growing plants. A deficiency is usually indicated by stunted growth and a purplish color on the foliage. Potassium helps to increase vigor and disease resistance of plants and is necessary for the formation and transfer of starches, oils, and sugars. It also helps to improve seed quality. A browning of leaves, weak stems, and a paucity of blossoms may indicate potassium deficiency.

Organic fertilizers contain both soluble and insoluble forms of nitrogen and phosphorus; most of the potassium is soluble. The percentages of nitrogen and phosphorus which are soluble and insoluble vary with the different kinds of organic fertilizers. Soluble forms of nutrients are directly utilized by the house plants and are available over the short term. For long-term release, the insoluble are released over a longer term because they cannot be metabolized by the house plant, but must be gradually degraded by soil microorganisms into soluble, readily utilizable forms. By using organic fertilizers your plants get both a quick pick-me-up and a constant supply of available nutrients.

Organic fertilizers can be over-applied or under-applied, although the chances of over-application are considerably less than with chemical fertilizers. I have already pointed out the reaction of plants to excesses or deficiencies of specific nutrients, but there are other symptoms of too much or too little fertilizer. Moss growing on the surface of soil can be an indicator of a lack of fertility or an acid soil. Green scum (algae) on the outside of the clay pots usually indicates an excess of nutrients. Excesses of nutrients can result in soluble salts forming a white crust on the surface of the soil, even with organic fertilizers. However, the amounts of soluble salts present with organic fertilizers at any one time are much less than with chemical fertilizers, because they are only slowly produced by microbial degradation. They do not present a problem because the small amounts deposited on the surface by water evaporation are easily flushed out by top watering.

Just as with watering there should be certain times when the amount and frequency of fertilization is reduced. Plants in a dormant stage or period of inactive growth during the winter, diseased plants, divided plants, and plants which have undergone root or top pruning require a temporary reduction of fertilizer. Plants in plastic pots require less fertilizer than those in clay pots because plastic is non-porous and nutrients are not readily lost by diffusion through the walls. As I have already pointed out, I use about one-half as much fertilizer with a plastic, ceramic, or other non-porous pot as I do with a clay pot.

COMPOST

Because compost is both a soil conditioner and fertilizer, it is an essential ingredient in potting soils. The aeration and water-holding capacity of the soil is improved by its addition and it contains approximately 2 percent nitrogen, 1 percent phosphorus, 1 percent potassium, and trace minerals, which makes compost comparable in fertilizer value to dry cow manure. Most of the nitrogen and some of the phosphorus are present in insoluble forms; they are released gradually in a usable form by the action of microorganisms.

I make "compost tea" for my indoor plants, but not in the usual manner, with a barrel or pail. Instead I brew the "tea" right in the pot—the flower pot, that is. I place finely screened or shredded compost on the surface of the soil to a depth of one-half to one inch. As I water my plant, I gradually leach out the nutrients in the compost layer to the roots, or trapping system, which then take up these nutrients. By putting it on the soil surface in this manner, my compost doubles as mulch and reduces the need for watering by slowing surface evaporation. Now, this is what I call "automated organic fertilization."

BONE MEAL

Another very important organic fertilizer (see Chapter 1 for amounts) which should be incorporated into potting soil mixtures is bone meal. When I repot an old plant, pot a new one, or replace a few inches of soil in a large established plant with fresh soil, I make sure to add a little bone meal—the steamed or sterilized form breaks down in the soil very slowly.

OTHER FERTILIZERS

If you use a well-prepared fresh soil mixture each time you pot or repot, the nutrients in the soil, the compost, and the bone meal should supply your plant with enough food for 30 to 60 days. After this time, however, these natural nutrients are exhausted by a thriving, vigorously growing house plant. Since it is rather inconvenient to repot every time the nutrients are removed, additional fertilizer, like fish emulsion, is necessary. To some, the mention of fish emulsion brings to mind a foul, fishy smelling liquid. At one time this fertilizer may have been so disagreeable, but not any more; today it is deodorized. It is water soluble and will not burn roots or harm foliage. Percentages of nitrogen, phosphoric oxide, and potash are roughly 5 percent, 1 percent, and 1 percent respectively. Since the nutrients are water soluble, they are readily available and quickly assimilated by the plant. Fish emulsion also tends to have a slightly alkaline soil reaction. There is another type of fish emulsion which is not as readily available as that described above. However, I do recommend looking for it because it is rich in phosphorus and potassium. (See Appendix for source.) This second form of fish emulsion contains approximately 15 percent phosphoric oxide and potash. I employ the fish emulsion at half the strength and half as frequently as the directions on the bottle state.

Another useful fertilizer is dry cow manure; it contains around 2 percent nitrogen, 1 percent phosphoric oxide, and 1 percent potash. Some people incorporate this manure into their soil mixtures, others make a form of "manure tea" from it. I think that making the tea is too messy by the bag and barrel method, so I sprinkle a teaspoon or so around my plants and let the water leach out the nutrients down to the roots.

Another good, natural fertilizer is wood ashes. It'll do

your plants little good to use wood ashes that haven't been kept dry, because any that have been exposed to water have probably had most of their nutrients leached out. Wood ashes should be used in addition to a nitrogen-rich fertilizer because they contain little of this nutrient. Wood ashes from a fireplace might contain 1 percent or 2 percent phosphoric oxide and 4 percent to 10 percent potash. I occasionally put a light dusting of my fireplace ashes around my plants before I water them.

While there are many other organic and rock mineral fertilizers with which we are familiar, I don't find them important for indoor gardening. The ones I have described here are fairly easy to obtain and are economical—they go a long way and are modestly priced.

In summary, my own program of fertilizing house plants is as follows: I put compost and bone meal in my soil mixes and don't use additional fertilizer for 30 to 60 days. Afterward I fertilize my plants with fish emulsion, at half the suggested dilution, occasionally substituting compost, dried cow manure, and wood ashes in the "tea-in-pot" method I described. When my house plants are actively growing in the spring, summer, and fall, I fertilize weekly, but during the winter I fertilize once or twice a month. If a plant becomes diseased or is severely pruned, I give it less fertilizer for a while. My method, however, is not necessarily the right one for you. You'll have to grow and watch your plants for a while—until you get a feel for how much and how often you should fertilize each one.

Chapter 4

Look Out for Insects and Diseases

Probably every house plant grower at one time or another has to deal with insects and diseases plaguing his or her plants. Although these troublemakers seem to show up no matter how careful you are, there are certain steps you can take to cut down on the frequency and severity of these outbreaks.

First, quarantine each newcomer and observe it for two weeks. If you don't notice any symptoms during this time, you can be reasonably sure that the plant is free of insects and disease. During this quarantine period try not to touch it and then to touch your established plants because you could unwittingly transmit a disease or insect infestation by contact. If it is feasible, thoroughly rinse each new plant with tepid water and a mild soap that does not contain detergent before placing it with your others.

Secondly, follow good sanitary habits with your house plants. Pick up fallen leaves or fruit, prune out dead or rotten plant tissue, and do not crowd your plants to such a degree that there is no air circulation around them. Leaving windows open without screens is just like sending out engraved invitations to all the neighborhood insects. Keep your plants in top-notch health so that they will be able to resist any destructive onslaughts. Wash each dirty pot with hot water and soap after removing a plant from it, and if you suspect a diseased plant was an occupant, a little bleach diluted to strength recommended on the bottle will not hurt. If you give your plants a summer vacation outdoors, give them a thorough rinsing and inspection before bringing them indoors. Of course, if a plant becomes afflicted with insects or disease, remove it at once from its healthy company. Then try to eradicate the problem in isolation.

What do you do, if despite all your efforts, some of your plants are invaded by insects or disease? Your first thought might be to spray them with powerful garden insecticides. I ask you to reconsider. Some insecticides and fungicides can be hazardous to you and damage tender house plants. The danger of some of these potent products is multiplied in a closed house during the winter. People and animals can be exposed to higher levels of toxins indoors, where the dilution factor is much less than outdoors. You might wish to consider some safer alternatives. In my own years of indoor gardening, I have been troubled only by a few mealy bugs, aphids, and occasionally, powdery mildew. Most house plant pests and ailments are not so severe to warrant drastic treatment. Let us consider some of the problems and means of counterattack:

Insects

1. For slight insect infestations and the removal of insect eggs, the application of a weak solution of soap and water can be a very effective weapon. This can be applied by spraying vigorously, dipping, or sponging the entire plant. Most plants, except those with hairy leaves (African violets, some begonias, etc.), can be treated with a tablespoon or two of a flaked soap like Octagon or Ivory dissolved in a gallon of room temperature or slightly warmer water (70° to 90°F). Some people add a few cigarette or cigar butts and let them sit in the soap and water for a day or two before using it. This solution is effective against aphids and scale with or without the tobacco addition, although the tobacco actually increases its potency.

Soap solutions should be left on each plant for an hour or two, then rinsed off well with tepid water. Such treatments, besides eliminating insects and eggs, also clean away dirt and dust which block breathing pores (stomata) and cut down on the amount of light reaching the leaf surface.

2. Oil sprays can also be used on house plants. Summer white oil (Superior oil, paraffinic base, viscosity of 60 to 70 seconds Saybolt) can be mixed with water at a rate of two

tablespoons per gallon of water. Test a leaf before spraying, because sometimes these oils can cause leaf burn or leaf drop on some house plants. They should not be used on gesneriads and ferns. Oil sprays should be applied at room temperatures and never in direct sun, and they should not be used more than once a month. Oil should remain on plants for a few hours, after which time it must be rinsed off thoroughly. These oil emulsion sprays control young scale, spider mites, and mealybugs with minimal hazard to plant leaves.

3. A cotton swab or paint brush, dipped in alcohol or nail polish remover, and touched to insects or egg masses of mealybugs or aphids can be effective. Touch the insect or egg mass only, since alcohol can burn tender foliage. If you get any on a leaf, wash it off with water immediately.

4. Pyrethrum and rotenone are plant-derived insecticides which are mixed with vegetable or mineral oil and sold as houseplant sprays. They control aphids, mealybugs, red spider and other mites, thrips, and white fly. Although they are reasonably non-toxic, some people are allergic to pyrethrum, and rotenone is very toxic to fish. Botanical insecticides like these operate as stomach and contact poisons against insects. I use these sprays only as a last resort against heavy, stubborn insect attacks. I've only had such an attack once in three years, when my indoor plants were invaded by aphids. I was able to take my house plants outdoors and spray them because it was relatively warm (above 60°F). If it had been cooler, I would have carefully sprayed them in a well-ventilated area—somewhere where I could have opened the windows. Because the oils in their sprays may harm some sensitive leaves, test it on one leaf before dousing the entire plant.

5. Cedoflora is another natural insecticide consisting of natural oils in a hemlock base. It is water soluble, pleasingly aromatic, and relatively non-toxic; it's effective against mealybug, scale, aphids, mites, and perhaps other pests. Oils in this spray may harm also some leaves, so always test a few leaves before treating the whole plant.

Usually house plants that are well-maintained are rarely troubled by insects. However, an open window or new plant might introduce an occasional pest. The most common pests are described below:

Aphids—These plant lice are small, pear-shaped sucking

insects about one-eighth of an inch long. They are usually green or black in color, although they are sometimes pink, yellow, or brown. They normally cluster at the soft, growing portions of plants and excrete a sticky, clear liquid (honeydew). Anyone who has a garden knows they multiply rapidly. Aphids favor the cooler group of porch plants over the tropical varieties. They are fond of ivy, geraniums, fast growing vines, dumbcane, gardenias, and ferns, but will attack other plants if these are unavailable. Leaf curling and malformed buds may be caused by heavy infestations. Use controls 1, 3, 4, 5, and repeat in three or four days to kill any newcomers and those missed the first time.

Fungus gnat—The adult forms, which are approximately one-eighth of an inch long, are delicate gray or blackish-gray fly-like insects that swarm near windows or fluorescent light units. However, it is the immature gnat or maggot that causes plant damage. These one-quarter inch long white maggots can damage roots, causing stunted, off-color plants. Adults can be controlled by method 4. Because the maggots live in soil containing decaying vegetable matter, using only finished compost in your soil mixes will prevent introduction of this pest.

Mealybugs—These insects have an oval, soft body about one-quarter of an inch long. They are slow moving, pinkish or white in color, and equipped with many leg-like filaments. Their bodies are coated with a powdery waxy material, which is somewhat impervious to insecticides. Egg masses look like cottony masses. Mealybugs suck plant juices like aphids, causing bud drop and sickly foliage. They may also infest the roots, especially those of cacti and succulents. In large numbers they can cause the plant to shrivel. The young, having not fully developed waxy coats, are more susceptible to control than the mature insects. Mealybugs tend to stay on the leaf undersides and exils of such plants as cacti, African violets, piggyback plant, dumbcane, dracaenas, gardenias, ferns, and philodendron to name just a few. For leaf mealybugs use any one of the five controls at 10-day intervals (except 2, which should be applied only once) for two treatments after disappearance of mealybugs. Root mealybugs are difficult to control. It is far easier to take a healthy cutting which has not come in contact with soil and to start a new plant in fresh soil.

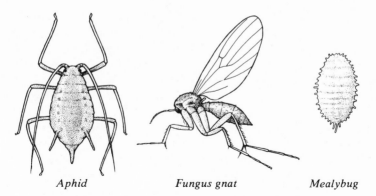

Aphid   *Fungus gnat*   *Mealybug*

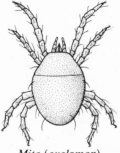
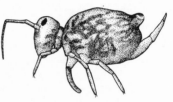

Mite (cyclamen)   *Springtail*

Scale   *Thrip*   *Whitefly*

Mites—Mites are oval shaped, eight-legged spiderlike pests that suck plant juices. They can only be seen with the aid of a magnifier or a microscope, because they are less than one-hundredth of an inch long. What's more, they are nearly transparent. Two mites—the Broad mite, which moves rapidly, and the Cyclamen mite, which moves slowly—are the principal enemies of house plants in the mite family. Incidentally, mites can be transferred from infested plants to healthy ones by hand or by plants in contact. Symptoms of their presence are stunted plants, malformed or darkly streaked flowers, curled or twisted and darkened leaves and stems, and failure of buds to open. The Cyclamen mites are particularly troublesome because they congregate in areas that are difficult to reach and suck newly forming leaves and buds and damage the growing tip. They prefer African violets, episcias, begonias, ivy, and cissus. The grayish, small, twisted, excessively hairy center leaves of infested African violets are typical of their activities. The Broad mite sucks on the underside of leaves and is more easily controlled. I suggest that badly or even lightly infested plants be discarded due to the highly contagious nature of this pest. If you want to try to control it, use method 1, 2, 4, 5, or sometimes a badly infested plant can be saved by immersing it in water maintained at 110°F for 15 minutes.

Nematodes—These are microscopic roundworms found in soil that enter plant roots and cause irregular swellings and lumps. Plants attacked by nematodes appear sickly and yellow, even when given excellent care. Extensive infestations can rot roots and eventually kill the plant. An infested plant can be saved by taking a cutting from it that is not in contact with the soil and rooting it in fresh soil. Once present, they are difficult to eradicate and can spread through films of water. If you know they are present in your garden soil, you must pasteurize it (see Chapter 1) or buy commercially prepared potting soil. Plants potted in garden soils enriched in compost tend to have less of a nematode problem.

Red Spider—These are small mites which can be barely observed by the human eye because they are only about one-fiftieth of an inch long. They have eight legs and are red, brown, or greenish in color. Red spiders suck juices and cause speckling and discoloration of leaves. If a plant is heavily infested, which happens quickly because of the rapid reproduction of the spiders, webs can be observed. Generally red spiders stay on the leaf underside. Since they like hot, dry conditions, maintaining proper temperatures and humidity can prevent their appearance on such plants as ivy, cast-iron plant, prayer plant, and red cordylines. Once they appear, use control 1, 2, 4, or 5—all at weekly intervals, except 2.

Scale—Only the young form can move, and these are most susceptible to control because their hard shell is not fully developed. Adults are one-eighth of an inch long insects with a flat, oval, or rounded hard shell. These insects, which suck plant juices and can cause stunting, are found on the stems and undersides of leaves. The color of their waxy, impervious shells is white, black, tan, or brown. Often the adults can be removed by hand with a brush or toothpick. Scales frequently infest palms, ferns, rubber plants, citrus, ivy, oleander, cacti, bromeliads, and screw pine. Try using control 1, 2, or 5, and repeat all but 2 at weekly intervals.

Springtails—These white or black insects, which range in size from microscopic to one-fifth of an inch long, can usually be seen when watering. They react by jumping rapidly about the wet soil. They usually feed on decaying organic matter and may feed on tender plant parts or seedlings. If they become a nuisance, try control 4.

Thrips—These insects are thin and barely visible to the eye. They vary in color from tan to brown, to black with lighter streakings. Like scales, thrips suck plant juices and cause leaf or flower damage by creating silvery streaks dappled with black dots. Leaves may fall and flowers may be distorted. Use controls 1 or 4.

Whiteflies—These greenhouse and garden terrors are equally at home with your house plants. Adults are white with wedge-shaped wings and an overall length of one-sixteenth of an inch. The young are small, cream-colored specks which cannot fly and are found on leaf undersides. Adults are usually observed when a plant is disturbed; they look like snowflakes or bits of paper moving rapidly about the plant. Since they fly, no plant is safe. Isolate the victim quickly. Both the immature and mature form suck plant juices, causing yellowing and falling leaves. The young are somewhat more immune than the adults to control and their populations increase rapidly, necessitating weekly control treatments for many weeks. Since whiteflies can become a serious pest, use controls 1 and 4 together at their first appearance. If you have a garden, and find whiteflies in it, be especially careful that you do not carry them inside on your clothes.

Diseases

Plants are also susceptible to diseases caused by fungi, bacteria, and viruses. Since it is easier to prevent such problems than it is to cure them, keep your plants in good health, maintain their proper environmental conditions, do not crowd them, and practice good sanitation in your growing area. Remember that diseases can lurk in fallen leaves, dead or dying plant tissues, and pots and soils of contaminated plants. Disease organisms can be spread through the air, by splashing water drops, by insects, infected tools, clothing, or hands. Disease-producing pathogens may penetrate plants through the breathing pores (stomata), wounds, or leaf and stem surfaces (epidermis). This penetration is aided by free-standing water on the plant, so avoid overhead watering or excessive splashing. A disease-infected house plant should be isolated, or better yet destroyed, before the disease spreads to your other plants. Avoid handling it and be aware of how easy it is to transmit the disease (see above). Do not save the soil, and throw away the pot, unless you sterilize it. To sterilize clay pots put them in a pan with cold water and bring the water to a boil; allow it to continue boiling for 15 minutes. Plastic pots can be sterilized by treating them with Lysol or Clorox according to recommended dilutions on the bottle. If you suspect a disease, a plant pathologist at your state agricultural experiment station or state agricultural college can identify it and advise you as to its seriousness.

Fortunately, with proper precautions, plant diseases do not constitute a major problem with house plants. In the last five years the only disease that has bothered my plants has been powdery mildew. Some of the diseases that can plague indoor plants are described below:

Botrytis blight—This fungus appears as a gray mold that causes stems, leaves, and blossoms to become mushy, brown, and rotten. If it appears, your humidity is probably too high and your plants are crowded (poor air circulation). Space your plants such that air circulates and dries plant surfaces. Avoid high humidity and do not over-fertilize (especially with nitrogen). If you use organic fertilizers (see Chapter 3), you shouldn't have any fertilizer problems. Remove and discard diseased parts. Mites can spread this disease, so check for their presence. Above all, do not splash water on leaves, especially on dark, cloudy days. If the blight persists, take a cutting from an unaffected part and root it in fresh soil. Destroy all infected plants.

Crown rot or root rot—This fungus causes wilting of the plant. If the roots are affected, they turn from their normal white to brown and die. Eventually, the whole plant dies. When the crown is affected, the plant will break away at the soil level with just slight pressure. Too much water and a poorly drained soil (see Chapters 1 and 3) invite this fungus. Since it is difficult to cure a plant with rot, it is best to take a cutting from a healthy part and to pay particular attention to how you water your new plant.

Damping-off—This term is a condition caused by a number of fungi and bacteria. It attacks young seedlings at the soil level, resulting in rotting, wilting, and eventual death to the seedling. Under proper growing conditions, seeds will not be damaged by damping-off. Use a pasteurized soil or sterile media (sphagnum moss, vermiculite, etc.; see Chapter 7).

Leaf spot—This fungus causes spots of various colors and sizes on leaves, that eventually merge into blotches and cause leaves to wither and die. Standing water on leaves, poor air circulation, and high humidity can all encourage leaf spot damage. Cut off infected leaves or take a healthy cutting. If the disease persists, destroy the plant. This leaf spot condition should not be confused with the leaf spots that appear on African violets after water is splashed on the leaves. African violet leaf spot is an injury, and not a disease.

Powdery mildew—This white, powdery fungus appears after sudden temperature changes, cold drafts, or excessive humidity. Good air circulation (do not crowd plants) helps to prevent infection. Such mildew can cause slight stunting of the plant, but not any serious damage. Take a cutting from an uninfected section and correct any of the poor growing conditions that may encourage this fungus.

Viruses—Some viruses, such as tobacco mosaic virus, can infect house plants. Plants that are infected have streaked, distorted leaves, ringed yellow spots, and appear to lack vigor. Viruses can be spread by insects such as mites. To my knowledge no cure exists. An infected plant should be destroyed immediately.

Chapter 5

That Nice Display
and What's Behind It

Just as no two homes are alike, no two plant collections are alike either. It is the individual's taste and imagination which can bring out the best in a display of house plants. As with any living thing there is a minimal amount of maintenance needed to keep it alive. Any extra effort improves upon the original. What follows is a little of both.

A view from the kitchen into the author's plant room.

The Pot Game

Sooner or later house plants require a change of pot and soil. When the moment will arrive is difficult to predict, but fortunately it is easy to recognize. One dead give-away is that root dangling from the drainage hole because there is no room left for it in the pot. In extreme cases of pot-bound house plants, the pot may even crack. Or perhaps a certain plant's watering habits have changed; instead of infrequent waterings, it has become an insatiable monster whose leaves droop and wilt at the slightest decrease in the water supply. This is its way of saying it is in need of a larger pot, since its roots have compacted the soil so much that water runs right through the pot without being absorbed.

Pot-bound plants may also show a yellowing and dropping of lower foliage or a decrease in leaf size. Some plants, while not pot-bound, may require a bit of fresh soil, or a complete change, such as cacti do about every two years. Whenever these symptoms of pot-bound plants occur, the plant grower must act to correct the condition. These symptoms are urgent cries for treatment, long past the early symptoms. The early warning signal is the extensive appearance of plant roots around the soil ball perimeter. This can only be observed by knocking the soil ball out of the pot, which brings us to that step. This procedure is also necessary for transplanting a pot-bound plant.

Basically, this is a simple operation. First you put your hand over the top of the soil, with the stem sticking out between your third and fourth finger. The soil should be damp to moist, so that it has some cohesion and is not dry and crumbly. Holding your hand firmly against the pot rim, invert the pot and give it a sharp rap on the bottom, or knock the pot rim on a table edge. Lift up the pot and you should be left with an intact soil-root ball. If the pot does not come away freely exert a little pressure on the crocking material through the drainage hole in the pot bottom with the eraser end of a pencil. If your pot was clean when you first planted it, you should have no trouble with the removal of the soil ball. However, if it was placed in a dirty pot, you will not get a clean separation. In extreme cases of pot-bound plants, you might have to take a thin metal spatula and work it between the edge of the soil and the inside wall of the pot. As a last resort, a well-placed hammer blow against the pot will release the soil ball and provide you with a fresh supply of crocking material.

If for any reason you must lay the plant and soil ball aside for any amount of time before repotting, you should cover the soil with wet paper towels, so that the root tips do not dry out. The pot you choose for repotting the soil ball should be one size larger than the first—there should be just about one inch of new growing space around the circumference of the root ball. Using a pot much larger can only lead to trouble: The plant will look undersized and ridiculous in a big pot. More importantly, the large mass of soil necessary to fill the bigger container will not be aerated and "worked" by roots for a long period of time. The unused soil will become soggy and cause trouble (such as root rot) for the root tips at the fringes of the unused soil.

You should be working with a pot that is clean and of the same type as its predecessor. A plant dislikes sudden changes in its life, such as would be caused in its water habits if you went from a clay to a plastic pot. However, if you wish to change the pot type (*i.e.,* moving from a large clay pot to a larger plastic pot for reasons of weight reduction), be sure to adjust the watering and fertilizing (see Chapters 1 and 3) to suit the new container. You should crock this pot to ensure adequate drainage. By crocking the pot, I mean placing of broken pieces of old clay pots or pebbles over and around the drainage hole or holes.

Place the appropriate soil mixture over these crocks to such a depth that when the root ball is placed on it, there will be about one inch between the top surface of the soil added later and the pot rim. This "headspace" is necessary for proper watering. After the root ball is seated, trickle soil around the sides of the centered root ball. Make sure the plant is not off-center, then gently press the soil around the sides with your fingers or with a flat end of a thin piece of wood. Give the pot an occasional good rap on the floor to help settle the soil into any air spaces you might have inadvertently created. These are not wanted since roots will not seek passage through an air space. Bring the soil up to, but no higher than, the

Repotting plants is a simple operation. Choose a clean, new pot slightly larger than its predecessor and crock it. Cover the crocking with potting soil, and then gently place the plant in the pot, being careful not to disturb its roots. Fill in gaps around the root ball with soil and gently press the soil down. Rap the pot on the floor to get rid of air spaces. Then water the plant liberally.

original surface of the soil. Be careful not to exert pressure on the original root ball with your fingers, for fear of root damage. Now water your plant until water runs out of the drainage hole. If you observe any settling of your new soil, add some more to bring it up to level. One last thing—wash that dirty pot from which you just removed the plant.

The Cut-up

Usually the beginning house plant owner eagerly seeks rapid growth of his plants because he feels that large plants are a measure of his success. Unfortunately, a counter-trend also exists; he feels the need to increase the number of plants he has. It becomes a feeling of the more, the merrier. However, this inevitably leads to a collision course called "I don't have room for all my plants." In vain he pleads with his mate, "but my plant would look so much better than the lamp on that table. So, who needs to read or see at night?" Eventually, a state of reason returns and the house plant enthusiast concedes that some means of limitation is necessary. Besides, he is tired of the snide comments of his friends such as "There he is, in his green jungle" or "Hey, you need a haircut and so do your plants."

In such cases, pruning may be the answer. Pruning can turn a creeping, crawling, untamed jungle of plants into a oh! and ah! collection. It can also improve the air circulation around those plants which were formerly crowded and intertwined, and therefore reduce the threat of plant disease and insect invasion. As you remember in Chapter 1, good air circulation prevents localized carbon dioxide depletion, which impedes growth, and localized concentrations of water vapor, which encourages diseases caused by fungi. Crowded, touching plants are great roads for the spread of insects and diseases, once these problems are introduced. And, of course, pruned plants allow a bit more room for a few more plants.

Before you begin to prune you must decide if the plant you have in mind can be pruned. Plants that climb or have vines can normally be pruned. So can plants that have many branches, each with a growing tip above a single stem, such as a gardenia. Plants that will not tolerate pruning include

succulents, which react to pruning with scars and deformed
leaves, or single stem plants such as cacti, which take so long
to mend that it is not worth the effort. Plants whose leaves
ascend directly from the soil level, such as ferns, are not amenable to pruning. A good alternative for those plants which
resist pruning is to take a cutting, propagate it, and start anew
with a smaller specimen (see Chapter 7).

There are three types of pruning. All are basically the
same—they differ only in their degree of severity. The most
drastic form is pruning back to old wood.

Because of the severity of this method, only a small portion of the plant—certainly not more than one-third of it,
should be cut at a time, or else the cure could be worse than
the malady. After the first pruned section recovers, you can
move on to the next, and so forth.

Ordinarily, this form of pruning is reserved for badly
neglected plants. You should not allow your plants to reach
this stage. You begin to prune by cutting off the leaf-bearing
portions of the stems so that you are left with a bare, woody
stub. In so doing, you remove the dormant axil buds at the
point where the leafstalk joins the woody stem. If you just
removed the leaves and not the stems, these buds would develop into new leaves to continue the photosynthetic process.
However, by cutting off both the leaves and the leafstalk axil
area, you activate a secondary set of inactive stem or eye buds
beneath the woody stem bark.

This activation of the secondary back-up system is a difficult process for the plant. It can be made less difficult by
enclosing the pruned area, after the wounds have dried and
healed, with a plastic bag. The plastic bag raises the humidity
which softens the bark and accelerates the emergence of the
stem buds. It is necessary, however, to let the wounds dry
before covering the plant with plastic. If the bag were placed
over the plant right after pruning, the fresh wounds would
provide a ready entrance into the plant for disease microorganisms. And once these organisms entered, they would
flourish in the humid atmosphere induced by the plastic bag.

A somewhat less severe method of pruning is cutting
back only to the dormant axil buds, or in simpler terms,
removing the young, leaf-bearing stems at a point slightly
above a pair of leaves. This encourages a plant to become

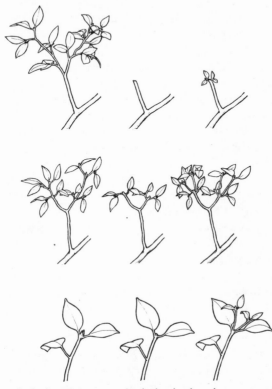

Three methods of pruning: top, pruning back to hard wood; center, pruning back to dormant axil buds; bottom, fingernail pinch pruning

bushier, because for each soft stem you remove, the dormant axil buds will yield two stems. Often this procedure can transform a spindly plant into a handsome specimen. Many of these pruned pieces can be saved to propagate new plants (see Chapter 7).

The least severe method is pinching off the growing tip of a stem. Pinching back in this manner will slow the growth of the plant and usually activate the dormant axil buds below the pinched point. This method, if used often and on time, is all the pruning you should really have to do.

Even with these methods of pruning, and the judicious use of repotting, some plants may get to a stage where you decide that they are just too big to handle. You are now confronted with two choices: either take a cutting, propagate it, and start off with a smaller version, or if you wish it to remain in its present container, prune it both topside and under. The latter might be just the ticket, if you just can't bear to give up the plant.

For the latter course of action, you will need a sharp knife. This tool should be given a special place with your other plant tools. Before and after you root prune with this knife, give it a wipe with rubbing alcohol to prevent spreading any undetected plant disease.

Remove the soil-root ball from the pot as already described in this chapter. Take your knife and shave off an inch all around the root ball. Do not cut into the heart of the root ball. Remove any pieces of crocking which may be entangled in the bottom of the root mass, and then repot the plant. Place a plastic bag over the plant to raise the humidity and in turn lower the transpiration or evaporation of water from the plant leaves. Since the damaged roots cannot absorb as much water as they could before they were cut, it is important to compensate by lowering the transpiration rate. Otherwise severe, and possibly fatal, wilting will begin. After a week, gradually open the plastic bag a little bit more each day to help the plant re-adjust to the normal level of humidity. When the plant has recovered, you should prune back an amount of top growth equivalent to the amount of root mass removed. Of course, this only applies to those plants which can be pruned. In time, your plant will resume its splendid form, but in a smaller version.

The Shaping of Green

At some stage in your enthusiasm for house plants, you may become dissatisfied with just the traditional display of plants in pots and wish to try some new arrangements like hanging baskets, terrariums or bottle gardens, bonsai, and topiary and totems. All these different displays require effort, some more than others. However, the reward is worth the trouble because they can help convert your shy greenery into a verdant work of art.

TOPIARY

Chances are you've seen some form of topiary in an outdoor setting. Maybe one of your neighbors shapes his hedges into massive walls, complete with ornate ball-capped corner pieces, or perhaps you've walked through a very formal garden where animal sculptures cloaked in green foliage transform the garden into an exotic zoo. Both of these are examples of large-scale topiary; indoors we must be satisfied with smaller versions.

The outdoor method of topiary, which involves training a plant to grow into a certain form, is shortcutted indoors. A wire form is placed around or under the house plant to give it support and a preformed shape, and the plant is gradually pruned and trained to conform to this shape.

You can bend your own wire forms from No. 8 or 10 wire or chicken wire mesh, but it is far easier to buy forms made especially for topiary. They are available in many shapes and sizes, including geometric and animal forms (see list of suppliers in the Appendix).

When choosing a plant to grow over a topiary form, don't pick a slow grower—choose one that has a moderate to fast rate of growth. Naturally, it should climb around the figure and have many small leaves to conceal the wire form. It should be relatively easy to grow and not expensive. Some of the plants best suited for topiary are climbing house plants such as small-leafed philodendrons or ivies, or even creeping figs. The ivy is best because it has a flexible woody stem which does not object to being bent around corners, and ivy comes in many cultivars, such as curly leaf or variegated types.

Starting a topiary form is not difficult. There are two methods, depending on which wire form you use. The first type of form, which is shaped from wire mesh, looks best covered with a small-leafed ivy, such as the needlepoint type. Into this mesh form, you stuff sphagnum moss which has the dampness of a wrung-out sponge. A stick is helpful for poking the moss into hard-to-reach areas. Narrow areas, such as the limbs or tail of an animal figure, are also wrapped with moss and then secured with rubber–or plastic–covered wire.

Now you take numerous cuttings of small-leafed ivy, which you have already rooted (see Chapter 7 for rooting cuttings), and insert them deeply into the moss. Secure them with rubber-coated wire bent in the shape of hairpins. Do not use uncoated wire or hairpins because these will rust.

At this point your patience becomes tested, but hang in there since the outcome is worth the wait. The ivy must be misted daily and fertilized every two weeks. Use the fish emulsion described in Chapter 3 and spray it on the leaves (foliar feeding), while lightly saturating the sphagnum moss. While your ivy is growing, you must pin down the new growth to conform to the topiary shape. Anything which will not conform should be unmercifully pruned back. During the summer, you may put your topiary outdoors to accelerate the growing coverage. After 12 to 18 months, your topiary will be lush, green, and well-shaped.

The other form of topiary involves a wire frame rather than wire mesh. No sphagnum moss is needed; the vine is trained to cover the form. You have a wider choice of plants with this method of topiary. You may use ivy, grape ivy, wax plant, Swedish ivy, and creeping fig (see Chapter 11 for more information on these plants). These forms are placed in the pot and their base is covered with soil. This base is usually counterweighted to prevent toppling. Plants are grown and fertilized in the usual manner. Recalcitrant vines are usually secured to the frame with rubber–or plastic–covered wire.

Keep the following in mind: Once the plants have covered the form, you must prune them at a frequency regulated by their rate of growth, if you wish to keep your topiary in a recognizable form. There is nothing worse than to hear someone say your green rooster needs pruning, when any fool can see it is a dog; or at least it was when it was pruned last. Also keep in mind that your topiary will not remain beautiful if you ignore the plant's environmental requirements.

TOTEM

There is another form of display called the totem. This is essentially a crude, simple form of topiary in the shape of a cylinder. You start with a narrow pole that is about three to five times higher than the pot. The pole, except for the part immersed in the soil, is wrapped to a depth of two or three inches with damp sphagnum moss, which is secured with non-rusting wire. The totem is pushed into the soil and a vining plant, such as philodendron, pothos, or ivy, is wound around the moss and secured in the usual manner for topiary. It is watered and fertilized like the other topiary forms.

SUSPENDED IN SPACE

No matter how much you prune and shape your plants, sooner or later you run out of room for new ones. Your house plants will grow and new additions will appear, every window sill and plant table will be crowded with your indoor greenery. But wait a minute, when this was the plight of many cities they found a solution—they built upward. This is our answer too; build upward by taking unused space with hanging baskets. And these suspended containers not only give us more growing room, they also beautify our growing area.

Hanging baskets, pots, container, and planters are normally available in garden centers, nurseries, pottery shops, and department stores. Some places sell them filled with plants; however, it is more fun (and economical) to buy them empty and fill them yourself. I prefer the ones with built-in

Hanging baskets are ideal for trailing plants like those pictured here. Such containers give plants more room to grow and give you more room in your plant areas by taking advantage of wasted space.

saucers because they catch excess water. You plant directly in this type of hanging unit; other ornamental types, made of brass and copper, serve only as shells to house separate flower pots. All are hung either from wall brackets or ceiling hooks; the hanging may be done with wire, nylon rope, wire, leather strands, twine, or chains. Wet, hanging units can be heavy, so the bracket or hook should be securely fastened. With bigger plants, I like to use plastic hanging pots rather than clay, because they are lighter and don't put such a strain on the hook.

Hanging house plants are treated the same as other house plants when it comes to planting, soil mixtures, fertilizing and pruning. However, the soil may dry faster in a pot that is hanging rather than resting on a table or window sill. This is because of the drying action of rising hot air in a room. Therefore, they need more watering, but not more fertilizer, because unlike soluble chemical fertilizers which are prone to leaching, organic slow-release fertilizers do not leach out as readily.

There are many plants suitable for hanging containers. Your choice is governed by the amount of available light you have (see Chapters 1, 2, and 11). Among those plants you might consider are ivy *(Hedera)*, grape ivy *(Cissus rhombifolia)*, philodendron, piggy-back plant *(Tolmiea menziesii)*, asparagus fern *(Asparagus plumosus)*, wax plant *(Hoya); Oxalis,* velvet plant *(Gynura aurantiaca)*, gesneriads *(Episcia, Achimenes, Aeschynanthus, Columnea, Hypocyrta)*, fuchsia, tuberous begonias, Christmas cactus *(Schlumbergera bridgesii)*, spider plant (*Chlorophytum comosum* 'Vittatum'), ferns, pothos *(Scindapsus)*, Swedish ivy *(Plectranthus)*, ivy geranium, and wandering Jew *(Tradescantia, Zebrina)*.

GLASS WALLS

Just as man has always been fascinated with a ship in a bottle, he is also of the same mind when he sees a garden inside a bottle. How did it get there? With a terrarium or wide-mouthed bottle, it is obvious. The following discussion will consider the various types of glass container gardening.

Glass walls around your plants may be bottles or large jugs, fish bowls, large brandy snifters, a glass apothecary jar, or a modern clear plastic container. When a large unit, such

All types of glass containers can be used for terraria. The container on the right is a half-gallon soft drink bottle that was cut in half.

as a fish aquarium is used, it is more on the order of a terrarium rather than a bottle garden. Just where the dividing line between a bottle garden and terrarium lies is not clear. It matters not; they all fall under the heading of glass gardens. I myself feel a bottle garden is a specialized form of the terrarium, which is more difficult to construct because of the narrow restrictive opening.

Types of plants suitable for glass gardens are many and varied, and they fall into three general categories: woodland, tropical, and desert. Since plants from different categories cannot co-exist in harmony in the same terrarium, you must choose your favorite similar varieties or plan to make more than one glass garden. For a woodland terrarium, you might want to consider the following plants: mosses, ferns, partridge-berry *(Mitchella repens)*, rattlesnake plantain *(Goodyeara pubescens)*, *Hepatica americana*, money wort *(Lysimachia nummularia)*, pipsissewa *(Chimaphila umbellata)*, wintergreen *(Gaultheria procumbens)*, strawberry geranium *(Saxifraga sarmentosa)*, violets, and small seedlings of trees such as spruces, hemlock, juniper, pine, and holly.

For a desert terrarium you could choose from many small cacti and succulents such as leafy stonecrop *(Sedum dasyphyllum)*, English sedum *(Sedum anglicum)*, many other small sedums, spiderweb houseleek *(Sempervivum arachnoideum)*, painted lady *(Echeveria derenbergii)*, Mexican snowball *(Echeveria elegans)*, *Crassula schmidtii*, and many other succulents as well as cacti far too numerous to mention.

A tropical terrarium might include various gesneriads (African violets, *Hypocyrta, Episcia etc.*), *Dracaena,* baby's tears *(Helxine soleirolii),* creeping fig, *Selaginella* and many other tropical plants.

There are many other choices for all three kinds of terraria far too numerous to mention. But remember when choosing others, you want a small, slow-growing plant, because some plants can run rampant in the lush quarters of a terrarium. If you decide to dig your own woodland plants, please make sure that they are not on your state's plant conservation list.

All three types of terraria (also including bottle gardens) should have an inch or two of drainage material (coarse builder's sand, fine gravel, bird gravel, etc.) as the bottom layer. This should then be covered with two or three inches of potting soil. For the desert terrarium, use the cacti and succulent soil mixture; in the woodland terrarium, use the humus lover's mixture; and for the tropical terrarium, also use the humus lover's mixture. These soil mixtures are described in Chapter 1. You will probably need a funnel to add these materials to your bottle garden.

Once the soil is added, you might want to do a little landscaping by creating a hill of soil and a scooped-out valley, a rock-studded scene, or a vista enhanced with small pieces of driftwood. Your only limitation is your imagination, which may be sorely tested in creating a miniature landscape where topographical features, background, and plant arrangement should all be combined to create a natural effect.

Plants should be positioned with their spread roots carefully covered with soil. Wooden tongs may be helpful in handling the plants. Narrow, long tongs are certainly needed to place plants in bottles. Other tools, such as a spoon and a cork on long sticks to dig and tamp will be necessary with bottle gardens. Once everything is in place the inside walls of the container should be sprayed with water to remove soil. The soil itself should be moistened, but not left soggy or watery and the cover put in place. If the opening in your bottle is narrow, no cover is necessary.

Desert terraria (no cover!) should be kept on the warm side and in a sunny place. The frequency and amount of water should be far less in this terrarium than in the other types. Woodland terraria should be kept below 70°F, and tropical terraria at about 75°F. Both should be kept out of direct sunlight. Exposure to fluorescent lights for 12 to 16 hours daily is very effective; such lighting also displays terraria in a pleasing manner (see Chapter 2). Overwatering in any terrarium can be fatal, usually by producing root rot (see Chapters 1, 3, and 4). In a terrarium the water transpired or evaporated from a plant condenses within the closed ecosystem and is recycled by the plant. Therefore, the plants maintain themselves for long periods of time without adding water. Any dead leaves should be quickly removed, because in the high humidity of any closed system like this they would quickly rot and possibly be the source of plant disease. If condensation on the glass becomes excessive, the top should be removed for ventilation until the condition disappears.

BONSAI—THE ART OF PREMATURE AGING

For those who have run out of challenges in the house plant world, there is bonsai, or what I call the art of premature aging. The actual translation of bonsai is tray planting. This living art of dwarfing trees and shrubs and growing them in bonsai containers is an ancient Asiatic hobby. Recently it has appealed to the fancy of many Americans. Before you get involved in bonsai, I must warn you that it can be a painstaking, time-consuming hobby.

When you select a plant, look for its bonsai potential. It should have a tapering trunk, interesting bark, some exposed surface roots, a minimum of three nicely tapered spaced branches with abundant twigs, and an interesting shape. Some possible selections for bonsai include: calamondin orange *(Citrus mitis),* dwarf pomegranate *(Punica granatum nana),* small-leafed figs (such as *Ficus diversifolia*), *Malpighia coccigera,* small-leafed gardenias *(Gardenia radicans),* rosemary, azaleas, beeches, flowering quinces, flowering cherries, hawthorns, Japanese maples, and evergreens like arborvitaes, boxwoods, junipers, pines, spruces, and yews. Select species of these plants that have small leaves, fruit, or flowers so that they will appear in proper proportion on a plant dwarfed to a height of 18 to 24 inches. The goal in bonsai is to end up with a natural mature tree in miniature.

Plants can be grown from seed, dug from the wild, or purchased from a nursery. For convenience and especially if you are a beginner, the best source is a nursery. Some offer trees suitable for bonsai, but I suggest looking in their junk corners. Often a misshapen plant, while unsuited for landscaping, is ideal for bonsai and can be obtained inexpensively in the nursery's junk corner.

Equally important is the selection of a container for your bonsai. Its size, shape, glaze color, and depth should be considered; it must be a complement to the tree it will contain. Containers should not be glazed inside and should have at least two drainage holes. Your first container should probably be inexpensive, because at a later date when your plant has a more mature bonsai look, you may be dissatisfied with it and want to repot.

Plastic screening should be placed over the drainage holes in the container itself. A layer of small gravel (*i.e.,* bird gravel) should be placed over this. Normally, the soil over the drainage material should be an all-purpose mix (see Chapter 1).

Now it becomes necessary to train your bonsai. First

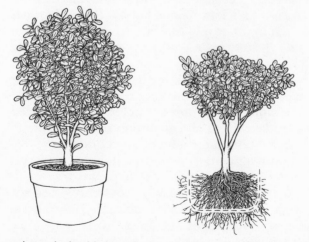

Nursery boxwood, selected for bonsai because of its triple trunk and its many twigs, is top and root pruned.

study your plant. One angle of sight will give you the best view of the trunk line. This will be the front of your bonsai, so to speak. The front and trunk line will determine which style is best for your specimen. These styles are formal upright, informal upright (slightly slanting trunk), slanting, semi-cascade (branches cascading over the rim and nearly to the base of the pot), and cascade (branches hanging over the rim and below the base of the pot).

Most of these styles, except the cascade, operate on the principle of thirds. The tree form is divided into three parts: The lower third or bare trunk, the second third or main branches, and the top third or dense twigs and foliage.

To achieve this effect, one must resort to judicious pruning. A careful study of various completed bonsai (pictures will do) may aid you in pruning. Horizontal branches are usually left in threes; one on each side and one in back give a feeling of depth and a dominance of the trunk line. However, these branches should not come out of the trunk at the same level, but be separated vertically. Branches on one side are often cut to be twice as long as the other side; this is to imitate the effect of prevailing winds. At any rate, the total width of both sides should not exceed the height of the tree. Foliage is sometimes left in puffs or clouds. Twigs should be left denser toward the top third to lessen the dominant trunk line there. Of course, it becomes necessary to root prune. Cut the main roots back about one third before the first potting. This will stimulate the growth of fine roots.

A second step in the training program is wiring for shape with copper wire (18-gauge). Branches and trunks are wired by spiraling the wire evenly around the trunk and outward to the edge of the branch and then securing it just tight enough to hold. Slowly and carefully the wood (preferably green wood) is bent to the desired shape, usually downward to imitate the drooping branches of a venerable old tree. Wires are removed after one growing season to prevent marking the wood. Most trees need rewiring; this is usually done at the start of the next growing season to give the tree a rest. It may be necessary to wire the tree into the pot at first, until it takes a firm hold.

After this initial pruning and wiring, the plant should be watered well and kept in the shade for a few days to enable

The pruned boxwood is wired into a pleasing shape, and after it has been trained in this shape, is repotted into a complementary bonsai tray.

it to recover from these shocks. Afterward your bonsai should be kept well watered; the containers are shallow and dry quickly. Insufficient watering can permanently impair the reduced root system. Use fish emulsion for fertilizing bonsai every three or four weeks, as they do in the bonsai collection at the Brooklyn Botanical Gardens. Repotting will be necessary every four or five years; a respectable bonsai specimen can be developed in five to ten years. Of course, it will be necessary to prune both the roots and top growth of a bonsai specimen (see this chapter for root and top pruning). It may seem like a lot of work and time, but what a conversation piece you will have!

There Goes the Dirt

With all things we must experience dust. So it is with house plants. They do get dusty, and there is nothing worse than dust-covered leaves for ruining a display of plants. An accumulation of dust detracts from appearance, blocks the breathing pores (stomata), and cuts down the amount of light reaching the leaves.

How do we remove this grime? On large-leaved plants you can take a soft sponge and room temperature water and wipe the leaves clean. If they are exceedingly dirty (shame on you), a mild soap such as Ivory can be used but be sure you rinse off any soap residue. It's a good idea to wash the leaves this way about once a month, although I am lucky if I do it twice a year. Smaller plants can be rinsed in the sink or shower with a fine gentle spray. It is preferable to clean leaves in the morning, as moisture left overnight on leaves can create ideal conditions for breeding plant diseases. Let them dry in a warm room out of direct sun. Plants with hairy leaves should be sprayed gently, so as to not remove the hairs. And do not forget the pots! A little water and soap will do wonders for their appearance. If plants could talk, they might say a clean plant is a happy plant.

Chapter 6

House Plants Keep Time
to the March of Seasons

The Green Rest

Maintaining a collection of beautiful, healthy house plants is a series of challenges. You have to maintain proper environmental conditions (soil, water, sun, ventilation, temperature, *etc.*), fight off insect attacks and invasions of plant diseases, and get through the traumas of repotting, pruning, and fertilization. If you manage to meet all these challenges, congratulations are in order—but, don't rest on your laurels. There is one more hurdle you have to overcome, and this is dormancy.

House plants undergo changes in their life cycle, just as their outdoor relations do. The period of dormancy in a swamp maple is easy to spot, because the tree looses its leaves and "rests" or is dormant during the winter. However, house plant dormancy is much more subtle. It usually involves a decrease in the life cycle activities, such as a temporary cessation of growth, or a slowing of the root system. These changes in activity may be difficult to spot; however, you must recognize dormancy and treat the plant in a different manner during this period. If you do not, your plants will slowly deteriorate, no matter how faithfully you care for them.

What triggers dormancy and how do you know when it starts? In nature, dormancy is brought about by a change in environmental conditions; it enables plants to survive during times of environmental stress. The best-known example is the loss of leaves on deciduous trees and the ceasing of evergreen growth when our northern winter strikes. But house plants generally come from warmer areas where dormancy may be the result of decreasing rain or increases in temperature.

House plants, because they are indoors, are not subjected to such environmental stimuli. Therefore, their dormancy response is limited or nonexistent. Accordingly, you are faced with two problems. First, you must recognize the symptoms of limited dormancy in those plants that naturally go into a dormant period, and learn to cope with the changes in culture necessitated by its advent. Secondly, you have to force dormancy upon those house plants that are unable to achieve it on their own. This might be required in order to be sure that some plants will blossom. Forcing dormancy seems like a lot of trouble, and perhaps you are asking why you should bother. The answer is that the key to success with house plants lies in the imitation of the natural environment. In their natural habitat, the hereditary trait of dormancy could be needed for blossoming, increased vigor, regeneration, *etc.;* ignore this pattern in your home and your plants will be the worse for it.

Some plants show obvious signs of dormancy when grown in the house. Their growth stops and their foliage deteriorates rapidly, leaving you with an ugly, withered plant. Plants in this category include gloxinias, achimenes, cyclamens, and caladiums. Other plants give less obvious signals; they just stop and maintain their present growth. If you look closely, you can observe that signal by watching the foliage growth pattern become static; that is, no new little, lighter green leaves are present, only larger, darker green mature leaves. Cacti and other succulents fall into this group.

With the onset of the dreary wintry months of December through February, light intensity and duration decreases. This may produce the more obvious signs of dormancy, which I described previously. It also provides a good time to induce dormancy in plants that do not show any symptoms. During these months I reduce greatly the amount of water and fertilizer that I normally give my plants. Plants in a dormant state can be damaged by too much water or fertilizer because they are resting and do not utilize as much water or nutrients as they do when they are actively growing. Do not be afraid to be stingy. If you are using artificial light, you should decrease it also. If a plant shows obvious signs of dormancy at times

other than the wintry months, I respond by decreasing the
amount of water and fertilizer I give it.

By responding to my plants in these ways I have not had
any trouble with the problem of recognizing or enforcing
dormancy. My plants are healthy and have been around for a
number of years. I guess they like their winter rest period.
Special cases of dormancy will be pointed out in the descriptions and culture of the house plants in Chapter 11.

WHO TURNED ON THE LIGHT?

Did you ever wonder why your Christmas cactus
bloomed at Christmas, or why it did not bloom at Christmas,
even though it was supposed to? It's because of photoperiodism, or the response of plants to the relative lengths of day
and night.

This response takes many forms. For example, plants
which require longer days than nights to bloom are called
long-day plants and those which need shorter days than nights
are correspondingly known as short-day plants. Plants requiring an even division of day and night are classed in an intermediate group and those that blossom under a wide range of
day lengths are called day length-neutral or indeterminate
types. Things would be fine if plant response could be clas-
sified so simply. Unfortunately, it can't. Those groups of short
and long-day plants which have an absolute dependence on
day length for blossoming, are known as obligate or qualita-
tive long- or short-day plants. Those plants which appear to be
day-length neutral, but which can actually be made to blossom
either earlier with short days or later with long days and are
therefore not absolutely dependent on day length, are known
as facultative or quantitative plants.

The complications do not end here either, because of
what I call a coupled factor. Temperature can also affect the
time of blossoming. For example, some plants will be short-
or long-day bloomers at a certain range of temperature, but
below this range they become day length-neutral plants. Of
course, there are more elements to the picture. But I will stop
here because most house plants fall into the day length-neutral
or indeterminate group anyway.

Exceptions to this category include kalanchoe and poinsettias, which are short-day plants. Other short-day bloomers are the Thanksgiving and Christmas cacti; however, at temperatures near 50°F they become day length-neutral plants, capable of setting buds anytime. These and other exceptions, as well as how to plan the time of blooming, is covered in Chapter 11 under each plant's entry.

Incidentally, it really is the length of the night, and not the day, which is the controlling factor in time of bloom. This influence of night was discovered after plants were categorized by day-lengths, so the above nomenclature is technically inappropriate. A good example of the effect of night length can be seen with the soybean, where light for one minute at midnight can prevent its normal flowering. Did you turn on your light while going to the bathroom at night and inadvertently illuminate your Christmas cactus during its critical period? Maybe that is why it did not bloom at all or not on time.

Finally, blossoming is not the only plant response affected by the relative lengths of day and night. Propagation can also be affected. For example, the living leaf or *Kalanchoe pinnatum* forms new plantlets along the old leaf edges on long days. Again, known responses of this type are covered in Chapter 11.

A Summer's Reawakening

When summer arrives, many workers look forward to a well-earned summer vacation. It is a form of rejuvenation for us; it helps us to regroup and start anew with vigor. Well, house plants are not any different in this aspect. They have awakened our dreary winter with their colorful dress of green and mixed colors, perhaps even some blossoms. After this faithful service, they too can use some rejuvenation, so that they can serve us well next winter.

Most house plants can be put outside in spring after there is no possibility of frost, or in early summer. Some plants, such as those with soft leaves, *i.e.,* African violets, are happier left indoors. The initial location of those put outdoors must be considered with care; it should be a deeply shaded location, such as under a large tree. This is to avoid a form of "sunburn" or sun shock; the intensity or available foot-candles of sun outdoors is far higher than that in a sunny window. Placing them in direct sun could be fatal. After a few weeks, they can be moved to their permanent position. Most of your house plants will do well in a semi-shaded area, such as the dappled shade under a large tree. A few, such as citrus, geraniums, and some cacti and other succulents, would do better with a bit more sun.

Do not set the pots directly in the soil, because they may become infested with various soil insects. I usually dig a trench under a tree and fill it with a few inches of gravel. Then I place the pots on the gravel and pile soil around them. This not only discourages soil insects, but also serves to improve drainage and prevent extensive root growth through the drainage hole. Never put a plant directly in the soil without a pot. Root growth will be very extensive; the plant will be difficult to cram into a pot; and if you do fit it by cutting roots excessively, you may lose the plant. Hanging plants may be suspended from a porch, tree branch, or patio in a semi-shaded location.

Plants outside will grow more rapidly than when they were inside, and they will require fertilizer and water more often to maintain this higher rate of growth. These summer outdoor months are a good time to do some light pruning and pinching to develop a bushy form (Chapter 5). It's also an ideal time to propagate any plants which have become too large to handle easily. (See Chapter 7 for methods of propagation). After the new plant is established, you can discard the large, uncontrollable parent. You must also keep a wary eye on these plants to detect any insects. Give them a frequent, light spray with a garden hose to keep them clean.

What if you cannot put your plants in a yard? People living in apartments or in areas where children and animals vandalize yards may have this problem. If you must keep them indoors, wash them with room temperature water (see Chapter 5) to remove the winter grime and pull them back from the window, since the intensity of the sun in summer is much higher than other times of the year. Let in as much summer air as possible. If you have an air conditioner, keep the draft of cold air off your plants. If you have a reasonable number of plants, you might consider putting them on a shaded porch or patio as often as possible, or preferably, leaving them there. This location is better than indoors, but probably not as good as putting the pots in the ground. At one time it was necessary for me to keep my plants indoors for two years. I gave them as much fresh air as possible. They did not look like a florist's dream, but they did survive.

Outdoor plants should be examined carefully as the fall approaches. Make sure you are not carrying any insects along when you bring them indoors. Prune back any plants which have become large or unshapely. You may wish to root these cuttings, if they can be propagated in this manner (see Chapter 7). Knock each root ball from the pot (see Chapter 5) and repot if necessary. Finally, give each plant a thorough rinsing with a spray from the garden hose. Bring them indoors about four weeks before you turn on your heat. This will give your plants time to readjust to your indoor quarters, so that they can tolerate the change of environment when the heat is started. Remember, frost will kill most house plants and temperatures below 50°F will harm many of them.

Speaking of vacations for plants, what do you do when you go on one yourself? If you have a collection of cacti and other succulents or a terrarium, you can just leave them without a second thought. But if you have other plants as well, probably the best answer is to work out a reciprocal agreement with a fellow plant lover who will plant-sit for you. Unfortunately, this arrangement is not always possible. Nobody plant-sits for me, so when I go away for a long weekend, I water my plants thoroughly before leaving and draw the curtains to reduce the sunlight. With this approach, I have left plants for three days without any losses. If you'll be away for longer periods, you must resort to the plastic bag trick. Water each plant thoroughly and allow it to drain. Enclose one or several in a plastic bag, using sticks to keep the plastic from touching the foliage. Seal the bag and put the plants in a place where they will not receive direct sun, which might heat the enclosed air to a fatal temperature. If a plant is too big for a bag, enclose the pot in the bag and wrap the bag around the protruding stem with plastic tape. Plants will keep for several weeks under these conditions. The only problem is that plants soon love the high humidity within the bag; you may even see aerial roots on some. Unhappily, insects and fungal diseases love it also, so make sure your plants have a clean bill of health before you subject them to this treatment. When you return, you must gradually desensitize your house plants to the house's level of humidity by puncturing the bag and gradually opening it a little more each day. There is a saving grace: you do not have to water your plants as you unpack your bags. Have a happy vacation!

Color All Year Round

Initially house plant owners are satisfied with just keeping their foliage plants alive, especially during the winter. Eventually, however, the lure of colorful blossoms beckons when outdoor growing areas become dull and dreary in their winter sleep. The following list of blooming plants may help you in selecting some seasonal color (blossoms or fruit). It is not intended to be all inclusive. See Chapter 11 for a detailed description of each.

Almost Everblooming
  (Begonia semperflorens) wax begonia
  (Saintpaulia ionantha) African violets
  Citrus—wonderfully fragrant flowers or unripe and ripe fruit all year
  (Episcia) flame violet

Winter
  Bromeliads
  Schlumbergera bridgessii (Christmas cactus)
  Zygocactus truncatus (Thanksgiving or crab cactus)
  Kalanchoe
  Euphorbia pulcherrima (poinsettia)
  Amaryllis
  Forced bulbs (hyacinth, daffodils, crocus, etc.)
  Primula (primrose)
  Cyclamen
  Pelargonium (geranium)
  Capsicum annuum conoides (Christmas pepper) colorful winter fruit
  Euphorbia splendens (crown-of-thorns)

Solanum pseudocapsicum (Jerusalem cherry) red fruit (poisonous)
Tradescantia (Wandering Jew)

Fall

Aphelandra (zebra plant)
Ardisia crenata (coral berry) bright red fall berries

In addition to blossoms and fruit for winter color, do not overlook those foliage plants with brightly colored leaves. Among these are prayer plant *(Maranta leuconeura kerchoveana)*, coleus, dracaena, dumb cane *(Dieffenbachia)*, variegated ivy *(Hedera)*, wax plant *(Hoya)*, crotons *(Codiaeum)*, devil's backbone *(Euphorbia Pedilanthus tithymaloides)*, aluminum plant *(Pilea cadierei)*, caladium, moses in the cradle *(Rhoeo spathacea)*, variegated peperomia, pothos *(Scindapsus)*, spider plant (*Chlorophytum comosum* 'Vittatum'), and strawberry geranium *(Saxifraga sarmentosa, "stolonifera")*.

Chapter 7

One Plant, Two Plants, Four Plants More

"My, what a beautiful plant; you must know everything about growing house plants. Could you give me a piece and tell me how to propagate it?" Ah, your guest has flattered you, and, of course, you *will* give her a piece to propagate.

Propagation provides an inexpensive source of more plants, whether it be for gifts, replacement of old, worn plants or those too large, or even for profit. In some instances, the propagation of a difficult house plant may be done for the challenge—what satisfaction there is in knowing your propagated plant took hold and is a new plant in its own right. And there is still another advantage to starting your own plants: A propagated plant establishes itself in your home, so it is conditioned to your home environment and may out-perform a greenhouse plant which must readjust itself to the less than ideal environment of your house.

There are two basic ways a house plant is propagated, sexual (seeds) and asexual (vegetative). Seeds are produced by the activity of the reproductive plant organs (pistils, stamens, and ovaries). Seeds are usually inexpensive, but require a great deal of time to mature. However, they do offer the excitement of creating new hybrids. Vegetative or asexual propagation does not involve the reproductive organs. It is done with parts of the plant such as stems, leaves, and roots. This method is more popular because it is simple and rapid, and usually reproduces the parent plant and its characteristics exactly.

Propagation by the vegetative method can normally be performed at any time of the year, although some plants are

84

easier to multiply at certain times. If in doubt, the best times are in early spring, when the plant is responding to the increasing illumination but has not begun new growth, or in late summer after active growth. It is a poor practice to propagate a plant which is approaching dormancy. Best results are obtained with a healthy plant about to start its growth activity, which is why I favor spring propagation. Unfortunately, this is also a busy time for outdoor garden activities, so you may find it more convenient to wait until late summer when your outdoor garden slows down. Seeds can be planted anytime, but I plant mine in the spring when I start garden plants indoors from seed; I have everything available and it just means a little more work.

Ideally, the medium for propagation should drain well, but retain moisture and be well aerated. It should also be sterile, to avoid the dangers of fungal diseases, such as damping-off. My favorite medium for vegetative propagation is sharp sand (see Chapter 1), which is obtainable from building suppliers or farsighted garden centers. It does require frequent watering and tends to be heavy. Other popular media include finely ground sphagnum moss, vermiculite (Mica-gro and Terra-lite), perlite (my second choice after sand), soil mixes, and various mixtures of the preceding components. In some instances water itself can be a propagation medium. My own preference for sand or perlite is based on their good drainage, aeration, and moisture retention, and of course, my good results with them. They are also relatively sterile as is, so there is no need to do any pasteurizing. They do not have a nutrient value, so they must be fertilized with fish emulsion (see Chapter 5). Moisten your perlite before using it, since the dust can be a nasal irritant.

For propagation by seeds, I favor the following system which prevents damping-off, but also provides the nutrients needed by the seedlings. On the bottom of a container, put a layer of sharp sand and cover it with a layer of compost sieved through 1/4-inch mesh screen. The thickness of each of these two layers should be the same and the top of the compost layer should be one inch below the top of the container. Cover the compost with about one-half inch of vermiculite (horticultural grade, one-eighth inch in diameter) or about one-quarter inch if the seeds are tiny, like petunia seed. In lieu of vermiculite,

you can also use finely milled sphagnum moss. Level this
material with a board. The vermiculite or sphagnum moss is
a sterile medium so there is no danger of damping-off. The
roots soon grow through the nutrient- deficient top layer and
receive their nutrients from the underlying compost. The sand
beneath provides good drainage. Under ordinary conditions
no supplementary fertilizer is needed.

As for containers for starting seeds, I try to recycle waste
products such as waxed milk cartons cut in half lengthwise
(you even have a choice of sizes), plastic food or freezer
containers, coffee cans, aluminum foil loaf pans, wooden or
plastic flats, glass jars (square mason jar on its side), plastic
shoe boxes or flower pots. One ideal container is the inexpensive plastic kitty litter tray. All these containers are also fine
for vegetative propagation. Containers should be at least three
inches deep to prevent rapid drying. Do not forget to drill
drainage holes in the container bottoms.

We are now ready for the various methods of propagation, whether it be by sexual propagation (by seed) or vegetative propagation (by parts of plants). The latter method of
propagation makes use of stem cuttings, leaf and leaf-bud
cuttings, corms, tubers, bulbs, rhizomes, rootstocks, division,
air-layering, offsets, runners, and suckers.

Starting Plants from Seed

When I'm ready to plant my seeds I prepare my container
of layered sand, compost, and vermiculite as I described earlier in this chapter. I gently wet the top layer of vermiculite
with the aid of a sprayer, such as an old window cleaner spray
bottle or a plant mist sprayer. Then I use a wooden strip
(one-quarter to one-half inch wide) to press rows or depres-
sions in the vermiculite at approximately two inch intervals. I
make the depth about three times the diameter of the seed, or
I just put a lightly visible scratch if the seed is very fine. With
great care I tap the envelope of seeds with my forefinger, so
that the seeds fall thinly and evenly in the rows. It is a good
idea to label the container as to its contents at this time. Afterward I fill the rows to level with vermiculite. With very fine
seeds I use a wooden block to merely tamp them into the

vermiculite. Then I sprinkle or spray the surface, and cover the seed container with a pane of glass (no glass?—use Saran wrap) to provide the moist atmosphere favorable to germinating seeds, especially the seeds of house plants which mostly originated in tropical regions. Afterward I place the tray in a dark place or cover it with newspaper. Most seeds germinate better in the dark; however, a few house plant seeds require light for germination (better house plant seed companies advise when light is necessary). Their place of germination should be warm because most house plant seeds require a germinating medium temperature of 65 to 75°F (keep away from cold drafts and windows). Again, better seed companies advise when there are exceptions.

Some of the following points may need to be considered before we go onward with after-germination care. Sometimes damping-off strikes (a fungal disease causing shriveling or soil line collapse of young seedlings) and destroys young seedlings. The vermiculite should be sterile, but if you want complete peace-of-mind, you can pour boiling water through the layered vermiculite, compost, and sand as a precautionary step prior to planting seeds. Sterile seed media are also available at garden centers. They usually require added nutrients, a disadvantage not found with the layered medium that I recommend. Sometimes a whitish gray mold appears on the soil surface during germination. It is harmless and disappears upon removal of the glass and exposure to sun. Finally, you must be patient. Some house plant seeds require a very long time to germinate, like certain philodendron seeds, which may lay dormant for a year before germination, whereas others germinate very quickly. Usually the seed companies give germination times (Park's seed catalogue is especially helpful).

Now back to our seeds and their germination. If you are covering the container with a glass cover, it is probably not necessary to spray the surface with water, unless it appears dry. It will probably be necessary if your seeds take a long time to germinate. When the seeds start to break through the soil, remove the newspaper and gradually remove the glass to return the humidity level to that of the house. Now the seedlings should be placed in a bright southern window or under fluorescent lights (try about three inches between tubes and seedling tops—see Chapter 2), and they should be sprinkled or sprayed gently with room temperature water.

When the leaves touch, you should thin the plants by cutting out the excess ones with a scissor, or gently removing them with a fine spatula and transplanting them. Just remember, each plant will require a separate container later. When the leaves touch again, you must transplant them to other flats or small pots. It is wise to sow your house plant seeds in the spring, so the young plants can be placed outdoors (see Chapter 6) after all danger of frost is past. Otherwise, you may end up with huge numbers of small pots and nowhere to put them. When the seedlings have about four true leaves they may be transplanted into appropriate soil mixtures (see Chapter 1) and treated like a house plant. Usually I make a hole with a flat pointed wooden label, lift the plant with soil by inserting the wooden label under it, place the plant in the hole, and tamp the soil around it with my fingers. Then I spray the plant with water and moisten the soil.

Truthfully, starting house plants from seed is a lot of work, but the rewards can be great. As a matter of fact, too great sometimes, especially when you find yourself with more house plants than you know what to do with.

I have grown many house plants from seed, some with great success and others with poor results. My favorites so far from seed are begonias *(Begonia semperflorens),* coleus, *Ka-*

Coleus and polka dot plants can be started from seed like these growing in styrofoam cups.

lanchoe, sensitive plant *(Mimosa pudica),* and polka dot plant *(Hypoestes sanguinolenta).* Good results can also be obtained with gesneriads (African violet, *Episcias,* etc.) and asparagus fern.

Vegetative Propagation

DIVISION

Vegetative propagation is used frequently and I propagate most of my plants in this manner. One of the easiest and most reliable means is by division of older plants. Certain house plants can be divided in the same manner as hardy outdoor perennials. Those that become eligible for division in their older forms include African violet, *Streptocarpus* (Cape primrose), *Columnea* (goldfish plant), *Aeschynanthus* (lipstick plant), *Aspidistra elatior* (cast-iron plant), *Sansevieria* (snake plant), *Asparagus plumosus* (asparagus fern), *Asparagus sprengeri* (emerald feather), ferns, *Calathea,* and certain orchids *i.e., Cypripedium.*

These are divided by severing or breaking apart the plant

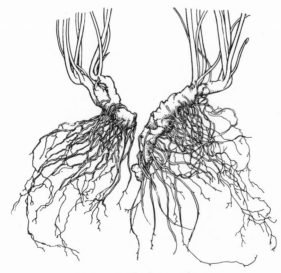

Propagation by division of roots

and separating the multiple crowns or roots. Each separate part is potted and grown as a new plant. Division can be a traumatic experience for the plant, so go easy on the sunlight and water for a few weeks. Severe wounds sometimes caused during division can be susceptible to fungal disease, so try to keep wounds small (cut in a narrow rather than wide part) and do not overwater to reduce the chance of infection.

STEM CUTTINGS

Another widely employed method of propagation is through cuttings. There are various types of cuttings: stem, bud or eye, leaf-bud, leaf, and root cuttings. House plants which can be propagated with stem cuttings include *Dracaena godseffiana* (gold dust dracaena), many jointed cacti *(Schlumbergera bridgesii*—Christmas cactus, *Zygocactus truncatus*—Thanksgiving or crab cactus, *Rhipsalidopsis gaertnerii*—Easter cactus, and *Epiphyllum), Tradescantia* and *Zebrina* (wandering Jew), *Codiaeum variegatum pictum* (croton), philodendron, *Pelargonium* (geranium), *Rhoeo spathacea* (Moses-in-the-cradle), kangaroo vine and grape ivy *(Cissus antarctica* and *C.* ["Vitis"] *rhombifolia),* fuschia, coleus, lantana, impatiens, *Scindapsus* (pothos), peperomia, *Hedera* (ivy), *Pilea, Aeschynanthus*

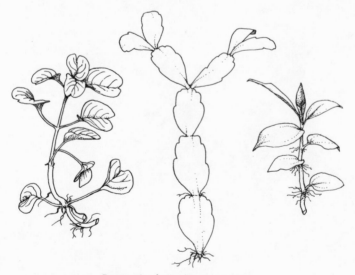

Propagation by rooting stem cuttings

(lipstick plant), begonia, *Abutilon* (flowering maple), *Ficus pumila* (creeping fig), gardenia, citrus, *Araucaria excelsa* (Norfolk Island pine), and some succulents *(i.e., Kalanchoe, Crassula)*. This list is by no means complete. Others are covered in Chapter 11.

Stem cuttings can be made with softwood or green plant parts; these are known as "slips." The young, vigorous stem tips of healthy plants are removed with a sharp knife, never remove slips with scissors or by pinching with fingernails because these methods tend to crush or compress the plant tissue at the breakage point. Take a cutting by making a diagonal cut on a main or side stem piece. Pieces from the end or middle should be about three or four inches long and contain at least two leaf stem axils at two different places. Quickly place cuttings in a moist rooting medium (65° to 75°F), such as sharp sand or perlite deep enough so that about one-third their length is buried.

Most will need increased humidity (especially gardenia, citrus, Norfolk Island pine) which can be provided by covering with an inverted glass jar, rooting in a covered terrarium or clear plastic container, or enclosing the whole container in a plastic bag. When enclosing them in these manners be sure to keep them out of direct sun. Waxy plants such as begonias, peperomia, ivy, pothos, and jointed cacti will not need the extra humidity to root. If you are not sure if your cuttings will need a higher humidity, either start off with the increased humidity or provide it when severe wilting quickly occurs. Keep the rooting material moist, but not soggy; also provide reduced light for the first week. Gradually—in four to ten weeks—the plant will root and as it roots you should increase the light, decrease the humidity (if covered), and provide a weak fertilizer. It is rooted when it resists a gentle tug. Pinch out the growing tip and transplant it to a pot.

Incidentally, many stem cuttings can be rooted in water (ivy, geranium, wax begonia, fushia, impatiens, coleus, dracaena, gardenia, wandering Jew, grape ivy, and philodendron) and will not require additional humidity when rooted in this manner.

Some house plants propagate better when cuttings are taken from more mature wood; such cuttings are known as semi-hardwood or hardwood cuttings. Examples include gar-

denia, citrus, and croton. These require increased humidity
and may require up to 20 weeks for rooting.

BUD CUTTINGS

Bud or eye cuttings come from that part of the stem
which contains growth buds or eyes. These cuttings are used
for propagating large-stemmed plants, such as *Aglaonema modestum* (Chinese evergreen), camellia, *Dracaena, Dieffenbachia,*
and *Cordyline terminalis* var. 'Ti' (Ti plant). To propagate, strip
the woody stem of its leaves and cut into pieces two to four
inches long; make sure each piece contains an eye. It's a good
idea to dust the ends with charcoal to prevent decay. Then
half-bury the "log" in a horizontal position in moist sand.
Enclose the container to increase the humidity and leave it in
a cool place. In six or eight weeks, when a callus forms, move
the container to a warm place (70° to 80°F, radiator or heating
cable on bottom) and keep enclosed and out of direct sun.
You can root the sprouts as cuttings or you can cut the log
around the sprout and pot it for rooting. This method is often
used with the stems that remain after a plant has been air-
layered (to be covered later) in order to produce more than
one plant from the parent.

LEAF-BUD CUTTINGS

Some plants can be propagated by leaf-bud cuttings, or
in other words by cuttings which consist of a leaf and part of

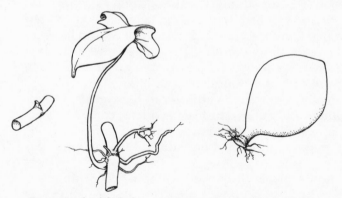

*Propagation by (left) bud or eye stem cuttings and (right) leaf bud
cuttings*

the stem. With this method, a plant grows from the dormant bud in the leaf axil, where it joins the stem. It is a useful method for producing many plants from a rare or expensive parent plant. Most plants which can be multiplied by stem cutting can be propagated in this manner also. The procedure is the same as for stem cuttings, but takes somewhat longer.

LEAF CUTTINGS

Another popular way of increasing the number of house plants is through leaf cuttings. These cuttings can be made in two ways. The first consists of taking a mature leaf with approximately two inches of leaf stalk and inserting it in rooting medium so that the leaf itself almost touches the rooting medium. The second consists of taking only the leaf or a piece of leaf containing ribs or veins. Triangular leaf pieces containing a portion of the main vein and the junction with a lesser vein are inserted half way into the rooting medium after severing the vein junction with a razor blade.

Propagating by both these leaf cutting procedures requires high humidity for success; a container or glass cover of sorts should be used. Cuttings should be kept slightly shaded and warm. Plants which may be propagated by leaf-petiole (stalk) cuttings include African violet, most other gesneriads, peperomia, many begonias, some succulents such as *Kalanchoe, Sedum, Echeveria,* and *Sansevieria* (snake plant), and *Tolmiea menziesii* (piggy-back plant). *Begonia rex* is the best known

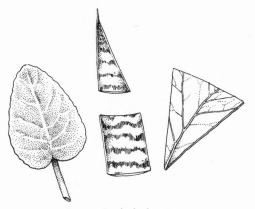

Propagation by leaf cuttings

example of leaf-vein propagation, although other large-leaved fibrous begonias can also be rooted in this way. Little plantlets form at the base of the leaf stalk or vein incision. They are separated and transplanted when they are about two inches high.

ROOT CUTTINGS

Root cuttings can also be used to propagate some plants. They are successful with plants prone to have root suckers, such as *Bouvardia, Plumbago,* geranium, *(Pelargonium),* bananas, leopard plant *(Ligularia), Clivia,* and snow bush *(Breynia).* Normally, in this kind of propagation, a piece of main root about one inch in length and containing a bud or eye is removed during transplanting or repotting. The roots, which are covered with approximately one-half inch of rooting medium and kept moist, eventually form adventitious buds and finally, young plants.

OFFSETS, STOLONS, RUNNERS, AND SUCKERS

Some plants can be propagated through offsets, stolons, runners, and suckers. These can be rooted easily under favorable conditions. These specialized shoots differ in the following aspects:

> *stolons* are thin, horizontal stems which emerge from the main stem just above or below the soil and root at the tip or joints. Fernleaf bamboo *(Bambusa multiplex)* forms stolons.

Propagation by root cuttings

runners are weak prostrate shoots which emerge at the plant base and root at joints. The Boston fern *(Nephrolepsis exalitata bostoninsis)* is one plant that has runners.

offsets are like runners, except they have a shorter stem. Offsets grow on the plant, hens-and-chickens, among others.

suckers are secondary shoots which emerge from a root or underground stem. Screw pines *(Pandanus)* forms suckers.

off-shoots are secondary shoots which start from the base of the plant. Some bromeliads have off-shoots.

Runners can be rooted by pinning down the plantlet at the end in a separate pot with a hairpin or wire loop. After they root, they can be severed from the main stem. Offsets (and runners) may be cut and rooted like a stem cutting. Stolons can be severed from the mother plant and potted as is, since they already have roots. Suckers and off-shoots should be cut to include some mother plant roots and then potted.

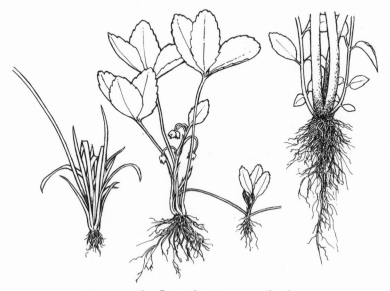

Propagation by offsets, stolons, runners, and suckers.

AIR LAYERING

An old means of propagation, air layering, is particularly good for multiplying the rubber plant *(Ficus elastica)*, croton *(Codiaeum variegatum pictum)*, dracaena, and dumbcane *(Dieffenbachia)*. To begin air-layering, take a sharp knife and make an upward slant cut halfway into the stem, approximately eight to 14 inches below the growing tip. If milky sap flows, soak it up in a paper towel; hold the cut open with a toothpick. Moisten and wrap a double handful of sphagnum moss around the cut area and hold it in place with twine. Then cover the moss with polyethylene tied closed at both ends with twine. If the moss starts to dry, loosen the top and add water. In two months or more many roots will form. At this point you can sever the stem and plant the rooted tip. The remaining plant can then be propagated—refer back to discussion of bud or eye cuttings.

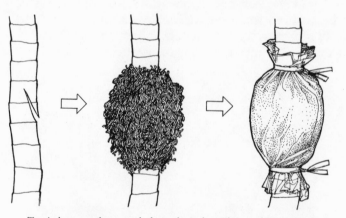

To air layer woody-stemmed plants, begin by making a deep, upward cut in the stem. Then wrap a thick layer of sphagnum moss around the cut and cover with polyethylene plastic. Tie the plastic securely with twine. When roots emerge from the moss, sever the stem and plant the new roots.

RHIZOMES, TUBERS, CORMS, AND BULBS

Another method of propagation is done with modified underground stem structures, such as rhizomes, tubers, corms, and bulbs. Examples of house plants readily propagated by

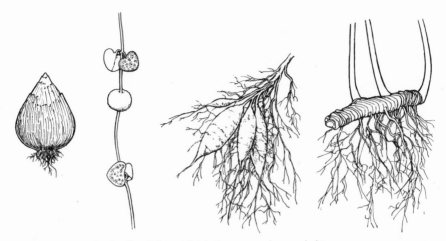

Propagation by (from left to right) bulbs, corns, tubers, and rhizomes

bulbs are amaryllis and forced bulbs (hyacinth, daffodils, *etc.*). Crocus are propagated by corms, and tuberous begonias and caladium are propagated by tubers. Rhizomes can be used to propagate Chinese evergreen and other large aroids.

Propagating with these modified underground stem structures is a one-for-one form of propagation in that you only get one plant for every rhizome, tuber, corm, or bulb you plant. There *are* ways for cutting bulbs into sections and getting more than just one plant, but they are tedious and lengthy processes, rather unpractical for the average house plant grower.

Little bulblets are also produced by large bulbs; these may be carried through maturity. Corms are similar in that they too produce little corms (cormlets). Tubers and rhizomes may be cut into pieces, each containing a growth bud or eye, in order to produce more plants. With rhizomes it is important to leave attached roots for food gathering, because, unlike tubers, they do not have a reserve of stored food.

Section III

House Plants and More House Plants

Chapter 8

Making an Indoor Garden
with Fruits, Vegetables, and Herbs·

House plants function primarily as ornamental decorations in homes, but some plants can do more than that for you —they can also supply you with food. You would be surprised just how easy it is to have your house plant and eat it too!

There are several ways of growing these edible and decorative house plants. Pots of herbs can be transplanted from the garden or seeded in the fall and cultivated indoors. Certain kinds of vegetables can be treated in a similar manner. A fruit tree like an orange tree can be bought by mail order and potted in a tub to reside on your patio in the summer and present its mouth-watering treats in your home during the dark of winter. The possibilities for extending the garden season all year round by bringing it indoors are endless.

Leafy vegetables and herbs usually need relatively less light than fruit or root crops, but all vegetables, fruits, and herbs appreciate high light intensities. A southern window, or at the very least, a brightly lit eastern window is a necessity. Even with a sunny window, some plants (such as tomatoes) benefit from supplementary fluorescent illumination. You might say that increasing illumination and improving your edible plant quality go hand in hand. If you have a sunroom or semi-heated glassed porch in a sunny location, you have the best possible conditions for growing those delectable, tasty house plants.

If you decide or need to use some fluorescent lamps in your sunlit growing area, you can use Gro-Lux Wide Spectrum fluorescent tubes. Since these fluorescent lights contain the necessary wavelengths for good growth and flowering, they serve as an ideal supplement for natural light (see Chapter 2 for more details on fluorescent lighting). The placement of these lamps will require some thought. For example, they may be placed horizontally for growing low leafy plants such as lettuce or herbs. The height may be regulated with a hook, chain, and pulley arrangement. But what if you are creating a salad corner with vegetables that all grow to a different height, like tomatoes, cucumbers, and lettuce? You can put the lamp in a vertical position. In this manner the tomato and cucumber plants can absorb light from both the window and the lamp along their growing axis. The cucumber can actually climb right along the side of the fluorescent tubes. Because the tomato and cucumber require high light intensities and do not mind some heat (do not let them actually touch the tube or ballast), the lamp can be placed close for maximal benefit.

Of course edible house plants must have good soil as well as illumination. Generally speaking, the soil should drain well and have a loose, crumbly texture. Most of the plants to be discussed at the end of the chapter will grow well in the all-purpose soil mix. As I describe in Chapter 1, this is a 2:1:1 mixture of garden loam, compost, and sharp sand, with one half cup of bone meal per peck of soil mix.

Keeping edible house plants in good health depends on proper watering and fertilizing as well. Be generous when you water. Let water come out of the drainage hole, but do not leave your plant standing in a puddle, because a plant with wet feet will cause you trouble later. When the top inch or so of soil dries, you can water it again. Vegetables and fruits are heavy feeders. During their active period of growth they may require a dose of fish emulsion or manure tea once a week or at least twice a month. I have found that in addition to these liquid fertilizers, a constant nutrient supply is beneficial. I place a one-inch layer of finished, sieved compost on the soil's surface. When I water, I brew a liquid fertilizer which seeps down to the roots. Meanwhile, the bone meal is slowly being broken down, assuring another continual, slow supply of nitrogen and phosphorus. The compost layer can be replaced about once a month. Be sure to reread Chapter 3 for more details on watering and fertilizing.

The atmosphere around edible house plants is very important, especially in regards to the temperature, humidity, and carbon dioxide content (see Chapter 1 for details). Ideally, the daytime temperature should be 65° to 75°F, and 5 or 10° lower during the evening. This night drop in temperature is very beneficial to plants. Night temperature drops are commonly experienced near windows. The humidity level may be a problem in the winter with some homes, if a humidifier is not present. Should your plants show symptoms of low humidity you can resort to some of the tricks for raising the humidity, mentioned in Chapter 2. Finally, the level of carbon dioxide around your plants is an important, but often ignored, factor in producing healthy vegetables, fruits, and herbs indoors. During the winter our windows are closed and the air is very still. Under these conditions, there is a localized depletion of the carbon dioxide around the plant leaves and because of it, plant growth is impaired. Try to place your plants where there is movement of people. On warm winter days open your windows slightly, but avoid a direct draft on the plants. You might even consider installing a small fan with an automatic timer to circulate the air around plants for short periods.

Some fruits and vegetables will be self-pollinating and others will not. If you have flowers, but they wither and die without setting any fruits or vegetables, you should try shaking the plant gently, but firmly, to scatter the pollen, or gathering pollen from the anthers with a soft camel hair brush and transferring it to the sticky stigma by contact. I have noticeably increased the number of fruits and vegetables on such plants as tomatoes, peppers, eggplants, and citrus fruits by helping with the pollination process.

In the summer your permanent edible house plants, such as fruit trees, will benefit greatly by being outdoors. Whether you place them on your patio or bury the pot in the ground, there is one important point to remember: Plants must be exposed gradually to full sun. Indoors you may have 2000 foot-candles of illumination at best, but outdoors, on a bright sunny day, there may be 10,000 foot-candles or more. Obviously, such an abrupt change would be a drastic and, more often than not, fatal shock. Start plants out in a shady spot and gradually shift them into a sunny area, or expose them to the sun for increasing intervals every day. You had better read over root and top pruning, because your plants may need it after a summer of vigorous growth (see Chapter 5).

Here are some edible candidates you might consider adding to your house plant collection. Of course, they will perform admirably in a greenhouse.

Fruits

Alpine Strawberry *(Fragaria vesca sempervirens)**

The Alpine strawberry, which probably originated in northern Italy, is a hardy perennial plant growing 6 to 8 inches tall. It is adaptable to pot culture and does well in a humus lover's soil mix. Unlike garden strawberries, it does not make runners; it is usually propagated by seed or crown division. It may be grown in 6- to 8-inch pots and produce fruit from seeds in three or four months (see Chapter 7 on seed propagation). Plants require about five hours of direct sun each day or 16 hours of fluorescent light (see Chapter 2) per day at a distance of three or four inches below the tube. Do not allow the soil to dry out; fertilize every two weeks. Varieties include 'Baron Solemacher,' the original Alpine strawberry; 'Harzland Alpine,' which produces bigger berries; 'Alexandria,' which produces the biggest berries; and 'yellow Alpine,' which produces, yes, yellow berries.

Apricot *(Prunus armenaica)*

Apricots are small, deciduous trees growing to 20 feet in height. They originated in western Asia and were introduced into England by a gardener of Henry the VII. In the early 18th century they were brought to California, which is now the center of apricot production in America. This species is not usually grown outside California, because its tendency to blossom early makes it susceptible to spring frost damage.

The apricot tree does well with the all-purpose soil mix. It can be adapted to tub culture with proper top and root pruning. Branches should be pruned back to encourage the strengthening of the wood and the formation of fruit spurs. The tree may be set outdoors when the danger of frost is past. It produces masses of pink blossoms (usually before all danger

*For an explanation of plant nomenclature see opening of Chapter 11.

of frost is past), which are self-fertile. If too many fruits are set, it may be necessary to thin them out when they are marble-sized to stand 4 inches apart.

The tree should be brought indoors again when frost threatens. After you have picked the fruit, go lightly on the water and force the tree into dormancy. On cool days (above freezing), you might take it outdoors to aid the onset of dormancy. During the winter keep it in a cool area, such as an unheated cellar, garage, or partially heated breezeway or porch where it will not be subjected to severe cold.

Some of the important Californian varieties are 'Royal Blenheim' (most common apricot in early market), 'Newcastle,' 'Nugget,' 'Perfection,' and 'Redsweet.' These are not very winter hardy. For tub culture in colder regions, varieties which are more cold hardy should be used. These include 'Scout,' 'Moongold,' 'Sungold,' 'Robust,' 'Ninguta,' and 'Sing.'

Banana *(Musa acuminata ["cavendishii"])*

Most bananas are too large for tub culture, but the *Musa acuminata* variety, 'Dwarf Cavendish,' is well-suited for this purpose. (Tubs should be at least two feet in diameter.) This variety, which came from southern China, bears 5-inch long fruits (up to 100 bananas per cluster) on a 6-foot high tree. The leaves are about 4 feet long and 2 feet wide. *Musa acuminata* is grown in frost-free areas of the south for its pleasant, yellow edible fruit.

Bananas require a rich soil which contains a high humus content (use the humus lover's soil mixture). Soil should be kept slightly alkaline with limestone to avoid banana fusarium wilt, which thrives in acid soil. Tubs should not be set outdoors until the evening temperature remains above 65°F.

'Dwarf Cavendish' is usually propagated from offsets, and the time required to bear fruit varies. For example, at evening temperatures of 65°F and daytime temperatures of 80°F, you may obtain fruit from the offsets in approximately 16 months. As the temperature increases, the time needed for obtaining fruit declines. Of course, this banana is ideally suited to greenhouse culture.

It will be necessary to prune surplus suckers. Initially,

only one sucker should be allowed to grow and bear fruit. When the plant is well-established and mature, you should allow a second sucker to grow while the first has maturing fruit. Large quantities of water and weekly fertilization will be necessary.

Flowers appear at the top of the trunk. The purplish-red colored bud, which contains many flowers, bends downward after emerging. This arrangement makes the banana unique, because the set fruit are then held upward in an awkward-appearing manner. After the fruit are set (no hand pollination is needed) only male flowers continue to bloom. These are now useless and, since they are wasting nutrients, should be cut off. The resulting fruit has a high sugar content and is rich in vitamin A, C, and B complex.

Barbados Cherry or Acerola *(Malpighia glabra)*

This shrub comes from the West Indies; it has pale-pink to rose-colored flowers. The bright red fruit, which is very high in vitamin C, is about the size of a cherry. It is well-suited for use in ices, juices, and preserves.

Barbados cherries can be propagated from cuttings or seeds. The shrubs can be kept about eight feet high as tub plants. They are quite happy in the all-purpose soil mixture. You may place the shrubs outdoors when the evening temperature remains above 60°F. Water it quite freely during the spring and summer, but only moderately in the cooler part of the year.

Brazilian Cherry or Pitanga Cherry or Surinam Cherry *(Eugenia uniflora)*

As would be expected from its name, this evergreen shrub originated in Brazil. Since it is quite tolerant toward pruning, it can be grown as a tub plant in the all-purpose soil mixture. It requires frequent watering and can be put outdoors when the evening temperature is above 50°F. Propagation is by seeds or cuttings.

Flowers are fragrant and white. The scarlet fruit is eight-ribbed and one-half to one inch in diameter. The shrub is usually a heavy bearer of fruit. Leaves, which are one to two inches long, are evergreen and glossy. Because of its attractive appearance, it is frequently used as a hedge in Florida.

The fruit makes an excellent jelly and can also be made into syrup and wine.

Cape Gooseberry or Ground Cherry *(Physalis sp.)*

The species of the *Physalis* genera are generally perennial and annual plants which grow one to three feet tall. These plants, which are related to the tomato (family *Solanaceae*), originated in South America. One species, *Physalis alkekengi,* is a well-known perennial ornamental called Chinese-lantern.

The fruit produced by the edible species, which will be described below, are very versatile. They may be stewed, eaten raw in salads, or made into preserves and pie fillings. Usually the fruit is protected by a papery husk. It may be picked unripe, and if it is, it should be allowed to ripen for some weeks before eating.

The all-purpose soil mixture is satisfactory for the *Physalis* species. They are usually treated in the same manner as tomatoes. Seeds are started indoors in pots or flats, and when all danger of frost is past, the plants may be placed directly in the garden or in large pots outdoors. At the onset of cooler weather prior to frost, they should be brought indoors to continue their bountiful production of fruit. A word of warning is necessary: Since they are related to the tomato, they are susceptible to verticillium and fusarium wilts.

Ground cherry *(Physalis pruinosa)* generally reaches a height of two feet and it is a prolific bearer of fruit. The fruit itself which has a grey-brown husk over it, is about one-half inch in diameter and is deep yellow when ripe. Jamberberry or tomatillo *(Physalis ixocarpa)* is somewhat taller, but has the same color fruit. Peruvian cherry *(Physalis peruviana),* or the true Cape gooseberry, has slightly larger, deep gold fruit.

Casimiroa *(Casimiroa edulis)*

This evergreen, a native of Mexico, is now found in California and Florida. Although it can reach a height of 30 to 50 feet, it can be adapted to tub culture with root and top pruning. It bears orange-sized, greenish yellow fruit, which have a slightly bitter, peach-like flavor.

In tub culture, it should not be placed outdoors until the

average temperature reaches 65°F and the evening temperature remains above 57°F. Fruit produced in the spring will ripen from September to November, but you needn't wait that long to harvest it. The fruit can be picked unripe before a threatening frost, and be allowed to ripen indoors with little flavor loss. These fruits are rich in vitamins A and C as well as carbohydrate and protein.

Since it is about as hardy as a lemon, it must be wintered indoors in places other than southern California and Florida.

Fig *(Ficus carica)*

This coarse-leaved, deciduous shrubby plant, a native of western Asia, is grown outdoors in California and Florida. It normally grows 12 to 30 feet tall, but is quite suitable to tub culture.

Many figs require a special wasp for successful pollination. This wasp, *Blastophaga psenes,* is not adapted to our northern climate. However, one species, *Ficus carica hortensis* sets fruits without this wasp. The best varieties of this include "Adriatic," which produces excellent fruit that dries well, and "Brown Turkey," which is also excellent, more hardy for northern regions and forces well in pots.

Figs do well in the all-purpose soil. Too much nitrogen encourages lush leaf growth at the sacrifice of fruit. The use of cow manure, compost, and bone meal has proved satisfactory for tub culture. It is best to keep the soil slightly alkaline. If the plants are grown in tubs, you can set the plants outdoors after the danger of killing frosts is past. It is the one- and two-year-old wood which bears the fruit. Root restriction will tend to dwarf the tree.

When killing frosts threaten, you can bring the tree inside and allow any remaining figs to ripen there. It is a good idea to rest the tree by enforcing a short dormancy after you have picked your figs. Use a scant amount of water and put it in a cool place, (35°F), such as an unheated cellar or sunporch for a few months. The leaves will fall off, but do not let this disturb you. In a few months (February) you can bring it back to a warmer, sunny area and commence watering to awaken it from its dormancy. If you stop dormancy by early February you may get two crops of figs by early September.

Figs are rich in calcium, iron, and vitamins A and C. They contain much carbohydrate and are known for their effectiveness as a natural laxative.

Kumquat (*Fortunella* species)

These are relatively small, evergreen fruit trees about 6 to 10 feet tall. Kumquats, which belong to the citrus family, are native to southeastern Asia and are slightly more hardy than orange trees. They produce small, elongated oranges useful for eating raw and making preserves. Their culture is very similar to that of oranges (see citrus, Chapter 11). They make excellent tub plants.

There are three species of *Fortunella; F. crassifolia* (Meiwa kumquat), *F. japonica* (Marumi kumquat), and *F. Margarita* (Nagami kumquat). The first two have spines, but the Nagami kumquat does not. The Nagami kumquat is preferred over the others because of its slightly larger fruit and greater hardiness. It is planted extensively in southern Florida. Like orange blossoms, its white flowers are pleasingly scented.

It is placed outdoors when all danger of frost is past; winter it indoors in a sunny southern window where its fruit will continue to ripen. Being evergreen, it may remain there all winter.

Kumquat trees are lovely and very fragrant when their flowers are in bloom. They require a large plant room or greenhouse, though, because these trees can grow quite tall.

Lemon* (see *Citrus,* Chapter 11).

Lime* (see *Citrus,* Chapter 11).

Loquat *(Eriobotrya japonica)*

This is a small evergreen which can reach a height of 20 feet. Loquats derive from central China and bear pear-shaped, orange-yellow fruit, which are one and one-half inches long. It is not widely grown in a commercial sense, but it makes an excellent tub plant. The fruit may be eaten raw or used in jams and pies. The seeds, being bitter, should be removed before eating. Its culture is similar to that of citrus (see Chapter 11). Place it outdoors when the danger of frost is past and winter it over in a sunny, southern window.

Orange* (see *Citrus,* Chapter 11).

Pineapple *(Ananas comosus)*

We are familiar with the ornamental bromeliads which make colorful house plants. But did you know the pineapple is a bromeliad also? It originated in Central and South America. In the United States it is grown mostly in Hawaii, and to some extent, in Florida. If you have a warm, sunny window you can probably grow this fruit in your own home. However, you must be patient, for it may take a few years before you pick your pineapple.

Next time you buy a pineapple, cut off the crown with an inch of fruit attached. Dry it for 36 hours and root it in sand or perlite (see Chapter 7) and transfer it to the humus lover's soil mix (see Chapter 1). You must get vigorous growth of leaves, if you wish to see a pineapple. Therefore, spray the leaves twice a month with a solution of fish emulsion. Let it run down the leaves and collect in the cup-like rosette. Like other bromeliads, a pineapple takes nutrients through the leaves. Keep the soil evenly moist, but not soggy. It should receive at least three hours of sun a day; it can also be grown

*As house plants these are equally as well known for their foliage as for their fruit.

Being tropical plants, pineapples should be kept in a warm, sunny area.

under fluorescent lights. Maintain the temperature around 72°F. You may put your pineapple outdoors for the summer when the night temperature stays above 65°F.

If your plant is two years old, and no fruit appears, enclose it in a plastic bag with a ripe apple. The apple produces gas (ethylene) which will stimulate fruiting. Remove the bag in three or four days. You should soon see signs of fruiting. If the stem shows signs of bending from the weight of the fruit give it some support.

Tree Tomato *(Cyphomandra betacea)*

This tomato is in the solanaceae family, and as such is related to the potato and common tomato. It is a tree-like woody shrub, which can reach a height of ten feet. Fruits are red, egg-shaped, tomato-like in taste, and three inches long. Temperatures below 50°F are not tolerated and the minimum fruit bearing age is two years. It is usually propagated from seeds in a manner similar to tomatoes. Use the humus lover's mix (Chapter 1) and water lightly in the winter. Put it outside in the summer when the nights are above 50°F and increase the water. Prune it to prevent a scraggly appearance. Once it bears fruit, it will bear for several years afterward. The fruits are fine raw, but are especially good in preserves and when served stewed.

Vegetables

Beets, Carrots, and Radishes

These root vegetables can be grown indoors with a moderate degree of success. You will need a sunny window or fluorescent lights. Keep the lights (16 hours each day) about 4 inches above the foliage tops. Carrots should be sown in a 5-inch or larger pot and thinned to approximately 1½ inches apart. If carrots are too close, they will not form good bottoms; pots should be about 7 inches deep to prevent distortion of the lower portion of the root. Better results are achieved with the short, squat carrots as opposed to the long, narrow varieties. Burpee's 'Little Finger' or 'Short'n Sweet' and Park's 'Tiny Sweet' are particularly good. It will take about 2½ months until you pick your carrots, but what a winter salad treat!

Radishes are also very easy. You can fit about 7 or 8 radishes in a 6-inch pot. Keep them moist, as excess dryness will tend to make them pungent.

Radishes may not form roots in the early winter, since they are influenced by the day length (see Chapter 6). In about 6 weeks you will be picking radishes. 'Cherry Belle' is usually a good choice. Beets should stand about two or three inches apart in the pot and will require about 2½ months to picking time. Do not forget the double bonus with beets; the tops are excellent cooking "greens" and the roots are well known as a culinary treat. Try Park's 'Golden Beet' or Burpee's 'Red Ball.'

Since it is hard to transplant these root crops without damaging their taproots, it is better to thin to the desired spacing when they are seedlings. Use the all-purpose soil mix and fertilize bimonthly.

Chinese Cabbage

For a winter salad treat, you might want to try chinese cabbage. It can be served like lettuce, used in cole slaw, stir-fried with oriental vegetables, or boiled like cabbage. Keep one plant to an 8-inch pot. Place it in a sunny window, or under lights; it will require almost three months to reach maturity. Chinese cabbage should be kept on the moist side. The best variety is 'Michihli.' Use the all-purpose soil and do not spare the fertilizer (give it a weekly dose of fish emulsion).

Cucumber

Cucumbers can be grown in a sunny southern window or on a string right alongside the fluorescent lights for full light intensity and heat which they need (70 to 75°F). You will need to transfer pollen from the male to the female flower with a camel's hair brush, if you want cucumbers. Cucumbers are heavy feeders, so do not spare the fertilizer (see Chapter 3). Follow the watering and fertilizing directions recommended for the tomato.

If you grow cucumbers under fluorescent lights only, you should be aware of the following facts: Cucumber seedlings respond well to extended illumination. In fact, they can even tolerate continuous lighting. Give them at least 16 hours of light per day. When they start to flower, cut the light back to 12 to 16 hours per day, because long day lengths can inhibit flowering of cucumbers.

Some varieties which you might try are Park's 'Cherokee' and 'Burpee's Hybrid.' It will be approximately two months before you can pick your cukes.

Eggplant and Pepper

Start your eggplants or peppers from seed during the summer by following the growing directions given for tomatoes in this chapter. For indoor eggplants, try Park's 'Morden Midget' and for peppers, try Burpee's 'Tasty Hybrid.' Eggplants and peppers both take longer to mature than tomatoes.

Lettuce

Lettuce can be grown under lights or in a sunny window, as long as the temperature is cool. Try growing yours near a window, preferably a basement window, for cooler temperatures, and supplement the natural light with fluorescent tubes. Place the tubes about 4 inches above the leaves and leave the lights on for about 16 hours a day. Lettuce should not be allowed to dry out; it must be kept evenly moist. Fertilize it with fish emulsion or compost tea weekly (see Chapter 3). Leaf lettuce generally does better indoors; try Burpee's 'Greenhart' and 'Salad Bowl.' If you want to try the heading type, you'll have best results with Burpee's 'Bibb' or Park's 'Tom Thumb.'

Tomato

The killing frosts don't have to mean the end of your home-grown, fresh tomatoes for the year. Grow a tomato or two as a house plant and you can pick them fresh throughout the winter. The results will not be quite the same when grown indoors, because the fruits will be fewer, smaller, and a little less tasty. However, they sure beat those rock-hard, tasteless golf balls they sell in supermarkets during the winter.

You will have to choose your indoor tomato variety with some thought. Sure you can try your favorite outdoor type and it will succeed to some extent, but probably not as well as the following choices. Generally, the smaller-sized tomatoes are better-suited to indoor culture. These are the mouth-popping or salad types we all know so well. For example, 'Pixie' is ideal for container growth. Other favorites are 'Small Fry,' 'Tiny Tim,' 'Red Cherry,' 'Sugar Lump,' 'Patio,' and 'Presto.' You might try something a little out of the ordinary, such as 'Red or Yellow Plum.' Perhaps you want a tomato you can slice for a sandwich. In this case, varieties which are bred for greenhouse forcing usually succeed better indoors than the standard garden ones. These include 'Tuckcross 520F,' 'Michigan State,' and 'Michigan-Ohio.'

After you have chosen your variety, there are a few ways to start your plants. If you have established varieties in your garden which you wish to grow indoors, you may cut off a branch and root it in water. Alternately, you can bend a branch to the ground, hold it in place, and cover it with soil. In about two weeks the branch roots and you can sever it from the parent plant and pot it. Of course, you can also start them from seed in the same manner as you would start tomatoes for setting outdoors. It doesn't matter when you plant the seed, but you probably want to pick your first tomatoes indoors when your supply of postfrost "greenies" runs out. This occurs sometime in November in Connecticut. To meet this date, you might start your seeds in late June or early July, or if you are rooting a branch, you might do it in late July or early August.

Once you have your tomatoes, plant one to a 10- or 12-inch clay or plastic pot, using the all-purpose soil mix. Place a stake in the pot; they'll need it for support later. Let them take full advantage of the outdoor growing conditions before you bring them inside. Carry them in before frost threatens or about two weeks before you turn on the heat so that they can adjust to your home environment. A daily misting and a shower bath weekly will help them get through their adjustment period.

The importance of light for the success of tomatoes indoors can not be understated. They require definitely a sunny, southern window, and the addition of a fluorescent lamp or two will certainly be beneficial. With 2500 foot-candles they will fruit abundantly; with decreasing levels of illumination there will be less fruit.

Tomatoes will need a biweekly dose of manure tea or fish emulsion as well as the compost and bone meal present already in the soil mix. Watering should be thorough; drain the excess from the saucer when you finish watering. Repeat the watering when the top inch or so of soil feels dry to the touch. If you do not have a humidifier, it might be necessary to mist your tomatoes or to keep the pots on wet pebbles during the winter. Of course, your plants will appreciate normal house temperatures of 70° to 75°F in the daytime and a 5°-drop at night.

Since your tomatoes are confined to a pot, it will be necessary to keep the top portion pruned to prevent excesses of top growth beyond the capacity of the root system. After a few flowers appear and set fruit, clip the stem a few inches beyond this point to encourage fuller side growth and to channel more food into those tomatoes. Let other blossoms set at a slow pace and remove some tomatoes if there appears to be too many at one time. It is better to have several good tomatoes over an extended time, rather than have many, miserable excuses for tomatoes in a short period.

You'll have to do the pollinating because of the scarcity of indoor bees. Gently, but firmly shake the plant to scatter the pollen; if you still do not get fruit, transfer pollen from one flower to another with a soft camel's hair brush.

Herbs

Anise *(Pimpinella anisum)*

This is native of the Middle East, of the area extending from Greece through Egypt. In its natural habitat it is a sprawling, two-foot high annual with deeply notched leaves and yellowish white flowers. The licorice-tasting leaves and seeds are a source of flavoring in soups, cakes, breads, salads, cheese, meat, and liquors. Propagation is best by seed. Sow the seeds outdoors, in a sheltered location in pots during late summer. Bring them indoors before frost. Since they transplant poorly, it is best to thin the young seedlings. Anise will succeed in a window having at least 4 hours of direct sun daily. Follow the general directions given for indoor herbs at the beginning of this chapter.

Caraway *(Carum carvi)*

Caraway, a native to Europe, is a perennial or sometimes biennial weed that grows to a height of two feet. It is of zone 2 hardiness (see zone map), and is found in North America. Leaves are compound with narrow linear divisions; they resemble carrot leaves. Flowers are small and white. The fruits, often mistaken for seeds by many, are used to flavor cookies, bread, and liquors. Leaves are sometimes used in soups or salads, and the roots can be steamed and eaten as a vegetable. It may be potted in the fall and used primarily for its young leaves and shoots in the winter, or its fruit, if it should produce any indoors. Culture indoors is similar to that already described for herbs at the start of this chapter.

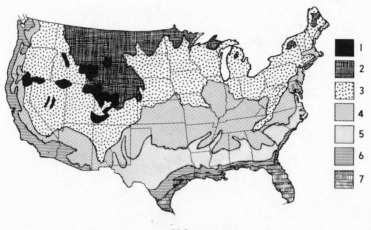

U.S. zone map

Chervil *(Anthriscus cerefolium)*

This is an annual reaching a height of 18 inches. It is closely related to the carrot, and has pinnately divided leaves. Flowers are small and white. It is native to southeast Europe. The leaf, tasting something like a mild parsley leaf, is a source of flavor in certain soups, fish, and meat. Although they transplant poorly, propagation is easy by seed. Chervil produces gatherable leaves in six to eight weeks. Treat it like the other herbs indoors.

Chives *(Allium schoenoprasum)*

This perennial, a well-known member of the onion family, originated in Europe and Asia. It reaches a height of two feet, bears purple flowers, and is hardy in all continental U.S. Chives are well known for their grass-like leaves, which, when chopped, impart a delicate onion-like flavor to cream cheese, cottage cheese, omelettes, sour cream, salads, *etc.* A clump can be lifted in the fall and potted for indoor growth at a south, east, or west window. New leaves will grow as fast as you snip.

Dill *(Anethum graveolens)*

This biennial, which is native to the Mediterranean area, reaches a height of three feet and has finely divided, threadlike foliage and yellow flowers. Since it transplants poorly, it should be sown in place. As a house plant, it is best treated as an annual. Sow a good number of seeds since germination is usually poor. Start them in late summer and grow in a south or east window. It will require staking. Dill reaches maturity in 75 days. Young leaves and leaf tips are used in meats, eggs, fish, bread, and seeds in pickles.

Lemon-Balm *(Melissa officinalis)*

This lemon-scented perennial herb, a native of Europe and Asia, now grows naturally in eastern North America. Being a member of the mint family (see mint), its stems are square and leaves are opposite and toothed. Flowers are white and borne on two-foot tall plants. It is easily propagated from seeds, cuttings, or division (see Chapter 7) in the fall or spring. Treat it indoors like mint, below. Foliage is used to flavor soups, sauces, and to make tea.

Mint *(Mentha species)*

Mints are perennial herbs characterized by square stems and opposite, toothed leaves; flowers are small and blue or white. The aromatic leaves are used in candy, juleps, jelly, and salads. They like constantly moist soil and frequent sink showers indoors. Mints require extensive pinching to stay bushy, otherwise they become scraggly. Try a south or east window. Pot small plants from the garden or propagate by division or from cuttings. Popular mints are spearmint *(Mentha spicata)*, peppermint *(Mentha piperita)*, apple mint *(Mentha rotundifolia)*, and field mint *(Mentha arvensis)*. Heights vary from one to two feet.

Parsley *(Petroselinum crispum)*

Parsley is a biennial (12 inches high) which is native to Sardinia. It is used as a garnish and a flavoring in foods and is excellent as greens. Fresh parsley is a good source of vitamin C, and when eaten after a meal, is a natural breath freshener.

It is easily raised indoors from seed (soak the seeds overnight to speed germination) and can also be propagated from roots (see Chapter 7). Parsley matures from seedlings in about 90 days. Keep it moist and in a southern window. It requires somewhat more high nitrogen fertilizer (fish emulsion) than other herbs.

Rosemary *(Rosemarinus officinalis)*

This evergreen herb, a symbol of love and remembrance, is native to southern Europe and Asia Minor and was probably introduced to America by the early settlers. It grows as a subshrub and has narrow, gray-green, lance-shaped leaves that are about one inch long. These leaves are used to season meat, poultry, and fish. Flowers are borne on upright spikes and are usually colored violet-blue. Although rosemary is a perennial, it is not hardy below temperatures of −5°F. Therefore, in much of the United States it is lifted before killing frosts and wintered indoors.

Lift rosemary and pot it in all-purpose soil (unless you are already growing it in a container) about two weeks prior to

Rosemary does best in a cool, sunny window.

bringing it indoors. You may also propagate it easily by starting seeds or rooting cuttings. Keep it in a partially shaded
spot, where it can adjust to the indoor environment. Some
leaves will naturally yellow and fall off when you bring it
inside. Water rosemary more than your other herbs; if the soil
dries out too much, some leaves will be shed. Rosemary does
well in a sunny window (east or south) with average house
temperatures, but it is at its best in a cooler area. While it can
reach a height of six feet under favorable conditions outdoors
in the South, it will not become this large as a potted herb.
You may prune it once or twice a year by cutting it back by
one third.

'Lockwood de Forest' is an erect growing variety, which
is popular in California. The variety *humilis* is low growing
and much more sprawling in its growth habits.

Sage *(Salvia officinalis)*

This is a subshrub (12 inches high) hardy to zone 2,
which originated in the Mediterranean area. Leaves are grayish-green and wrinkled. Pot up a young plant or propagate it
from seed, cuttings, or by division. Give it a half day of sun
indoors and keep it moist. Leaves are minced for flavoring in
cheese, pickles, sausage, veal, pork, and chicken. Dried and
powdered leaves are used in poultry or meat stuffings.

Sweet Basil *(Ocimum basilicum)*

Sweet basil is an annual reaching a height of two feet. It
is native to tropical Asia. Leaves are oval, opposite and purple
and flowers are white to purplish. It is easily propagated by
seeds (60 days to picking) or cuttings. It has been said that in
the house as a pot plant, it keeps away house flies. Fresh leaves
are excellent seasoning for meats, salads, eggs, and vegetables
(especially potatoes and tomatoes). Keep a pot of sweet basil
in a sunny southern or eastern window, mist it frequently, and
keep picking those leaves. In this manner it will last a year
indoors. There is a miniature sweet basil, (10 inches high)
Ocimum minimum, which is particularly well-suited to growth
under fluorescent lights.

Sweet Marjoram *(Majorana hortensis)*

This perennial, usually treated as an annual because it dies easily in winter, reaches a height of two feet. It is native to Europe. Leaves are grayish-green and flowers are whitish to purplish. Soups, salad dressings, stuffings, eggs, and meat (herb coatings) can be seasoned with the leaves. It is easily propagated from seeds and from cuttings. Keep it evenly moist in a bright southern window. You may start picking leaves when the plant is four inches high.

Tarragon *(Artemisia dracunculus)*

This perennial herb, native to southern Russia, grows to two feet and is winter hardy to the southern most extremities of zone 3. Leaves are long, alternate, and narrow; flowers are greenish white. Leaves are used to flavor salads, fish, sauce, and confectionary. A vinegar called tarragon vinegar is made from the leaves and white vinegar. Propagate it from cuttings or by division. Keep it in a southern window. Keep the soil on the dry side.

Common Thyme *(Thymus vulgaris)*

This low or ground cover herb is a hardy perennial in areas where temperatures do not drop below $-10°F$. It has small (one-half inch long), evergreen, pungent leaves used to season meat, poultry, and vegetable dishes, and tiny lilac to purplish colored flowers, which are carried on upright spikes. Common thyme, native to southern Europe, grows ideally in rock gardens and alongside border walks. Golden thyme *(Thymus vulgarus aureus)* is a variety of common thyme which has golden-blotched foliage; it has both culinary and ornamental value. Another species of *Thymus,* Sicily thyme *(Thymus nitidus),* is also used as an herb; it is added to poultry seasoning. It has about the same degree of hardiness as common thyme.

Thyme can be grown in pots from cuttings or seeds in an all-purpose soil mixture. In fact it will be necessary to winter it indoors in the less mild northern, central, and western states. It requires the same growing conditions as rosemary, but should be allowed to dry out a bit more between waterings.

The common thyme plant here has grey-green leaves. For best flavor and aroma pick them before the pink or violet flowers appear.

Winter Savory *(Satureja montana)*

This shrubby perennial herb reaches a height of 15 inches and is winter hardy to the southernmost extremities of zone 3. It is native to Europe. Fresh leaves are used to season green vegetables; dried leaves are used to season meats, vegetables (cabbage and turnips), salad dressings, and dips. Propagation is by seeds, cuttings, and division. Keep it on the dry side in a southern window.

Chapter 9

The Winter Comes Alive
with Forced Bulbs

Do you have the winter doldrums? Are you tired of winter's drab colors, and find that your colorful house plants just do not help to brighten things up enough for you in January or February? Then what you need are some colorful harbingers of spring, such as crocus, hyacinths, daffodils, *etc.* Yes, you say, but it is winter, not spring. Well then, let us make it spring indoors. How? Simple, we can force the spring bulbs into bloom indoors. Forcing bulbs requires a minimum of effort, but the rewards are sheer dazzle. That's my kind of indoor gardening.

When you purchase your bulbs, whether it be by mail or from a garden center, get the largest grade. The little extra investment is returned several-fold, since this grade gives the best and most stunning flowers. These bulbs should have a paper-like skin; if it has been rubbed off, these bulbs were probably handled very roughly and are possibly damaged. If so, they'll have poor blooms. The bottom flat portion of the bulb (basal plate) should be uninjured, since all the roots must come from it.

Usually you'll purchase the bulbs before you are ready to use them, especially if you want a good choice. This may present you with a problem of storage. Bulbs may not be left in a hot, dry place, because they will deteriorate. They draw upon their internal moisture for survival during dormancy. I think the best thing is to put them in a perforated plastic bag, such as the kind oranges are purchased in, or in a perforated paper bag, and store them in the vegetable crisper of your refrigerator. Don't let them get wet; if you do they could

122

*Daffodils and hyacinths, like the ones pictured here,
as well as crocus, can be forced indoors for early
blooms.*

develop bulb rot. Of course, do not expose them to bright
light, or premature sprouting will result; once this occurs, the
bulbs usually blast (no flower bud emerges). Ordinary light
encountered by opening the crisper is not sufficient to cause
any problems.

I plant my bulbs for forcing in late October or early
November. My favorite containers are the clay or plastic pots
designed for bulbs; these containers are more squat than the
ordinary pot and are appropriately called bulb pans. On hand
I also have crocks (broken clay pot shards), all-purpose soil
mixture, water, a garden trowel or very large spoon, and
labels.

Step-by-Step to Bulb Forcing

The following method can be used to force most spring
flowering bulbs. Any variations or pertinent facts will be discussed in the brief bulb descriptions which will follow. Often
some bulbs can be forced in only water and pebbles; this
method of forcing will be described also.

Cover the bottom of the pot (especially the drainage

hole) with the crocks. This prevents the soil from being washed out the pot and allows air entry, which is needed for good root development. Next, fill the pot with soil, leaving a headspace equal to the height of the bulb plus one inch. For example, if the bulb is one and one-half inches long, you should bring the soil to within two and one-half inches of the top of the pot. The soil should also be at least one inch deep. Once this is done, the soil should be leveled off and the bulbs placed on top of it. You may put them as close as possible, as long as they do not touch one another. Bulbs already contain enough stored nourishment to carry them through the blooming stage, so do not worry about close spacing. As an example, you can put six large tulip bulbs (five in an outside circle and one in the center) in one 8-inch bulb pan. Work some soil around the bulbs and cover them so that only their tips show. This will leave about one inch of head space above the soil. Label the bulbs and give them a thorough watering so that water comes out of the drainage hole.

Now comes the (dark) cold treatment period. In their natural environment, bulbs are subjected to a winter cold period, so indoors we must supply the low temperatures. The importance of this dark, cold treatment should not be underestimated. The massive root systems, which are necessary for proper top growth would develop in cold or warm temperatures, but the embryonic flower bud would not develop without this cold treatment.

There are four obvious ways to supply the dark, cold period, although you may think of more. One of the easiest is to store the pots in a refrigerator (preferably that old one in the cellar). I am lucky and have access to a large walk-in refrigerator. The temperature should be around 38°F, and if the area is brightly lit, cover the bulbs—perhaps put them in a cardboard box with a lid. In a cellar refrigerator, you can put them on the shelves as is and disconnect the refrigerator light bulb. Alternately you can put them in a glass-covered cold frame, put an inverted pot over the bulb pans, and then cover them with eight inches of hay, dry leaves, or peat moss. Storage in an unheated garage or porch is also feasible. Place the pots in a covered box filled at least six inches deep with packing excelsior (styrofoam chips are also excellent) and leave the

Bulb pans are especially good for forcing bulbs. Crock the drainage hole and cover the crocking with a level layer of soil. Place the bulbs as close together as possible without contact on top of the soil and cover with more soil so that only the tips show. Label the pot and water thoroughly before beginning the cold treatment.

box closed. You may cover the boxes with burlap. Or you can dig a trench about eight inches deep, place the pots in it, and cover them with ten inches of soil, then six inches of hay to prevent heaving of the ground. I do not like the last method, because a pickaxe is usually needed to get the pots out of the frozen soil.

During this period the bulbs must not dry out: you will lose them if they do. If you are storing them in a refrigerator, you can simply open the door and check them. However, in boxes in coldframes or garages, it is not as easy. A very simple way to make certain that they won't dry out is to put the pots into a plastic dry-cleaning bag before covering them. The cool temperature plus the plastic enclosure will prevent drying. Undoubtedly you will notice a heavy growth of fuzzy, dirty-gray mold on the soil surface. Do not worry: it is harmless and will disappear when the bulbs are brought into the sun.

These bulbs will require about six weeks of cold treatment before they will start rooting. When they are ready you will sometimes have roots emerging from the drainage hole and definite white sprouts at the bulb tips. If in doubt, you can knock out the soil ball (see Chapter 5); you should see a tangle of white roots encircling the soil ball. Even if they are ready, you can leave some of them in cold treatment and bring them out at ten-day intervals for a succession of bloom.

Now comes an important step. The bulbs must be put in a cool place, and not in direct sun. Temperatures should be about 50° to 55°F. If the temperature is higher, the buds may open before they clear the foliage. The best place might be a north cellar window sill or semi-heated porch or breezeway. When the white growing tip turns green, move them to a sunny cool window (or try about 10 inches below fluorescent tubes) where daytime temperatures are 60° to 65°F and a 5- or 10-degree night drop in temperature occurs. A southern cellar window is ideal. Do not forget to keep them watered.

When the buds begin to open, bring them into the room where you wish them to bloom. Keeping the blossoms out of direct sunlight will prolong the blooms and preserve the color and fragrance. If you keep your house at 68° or 70°F, and drop the temperature a few degrees at night, your blossoms will also last longer. They may require staking and you must keep an eye on the watering.

When sprouts begin to emerge from the tips, take the bulbs from the cold treatment area and place them in a cool, semi-shaded place.

Do not throw them away when they are finished blooming. Cut off the dead blossoms and put them in a sunny cool window, such as in the cellar. Keep them watered. When the weather warms up, plant them in your garden at the proper depth and be generous with the bone meal. They may not bloom the next year, or they may be skimpy blossoms, since forcing is a rough experience for the bulb. However, with generous helpings of bone meal, they will recover.

Bulbs, such as hyacinths, crocus, and paper white narcissus can also be forced into bloom in water. Paper white narcissus are usually put into a container on top of a layer of moist pebbles about two or three inches deep. These are kept wet and treated to the same conditions as the potted bulbs. However, since they are cold pretreated and are only half-hardy, the root formation temperature should be kept around 50°F.

Alternately you can grow them in commercially prepared bulb fiber, or homemade fiber made from your own shredded peatmoss plus a sprinkle of ground limestone to counteract the acidity of the peatmoss. It should be kept damp. The fiber has one advantage in that it supports stakes (pebbles do not), which are usually needed for paper whites. One year I grew paper whites in moist sand and had good results.

Crocus and hyacinths can also be grown in water in spe-

Growing glasses, like the one pictured here,
are specially designed for bulbs.

cially made glass bulb containers. These bulb glasses have a constriction near the top on which the bulb rests. Water is added to the bottom section so that it just touches the bottom of the bulb. A dash of charcoal can be added to the water to keep it fresh. Bulbs forced in these glasses should be treated in the same manner as that described for the potted bulbs. Keep your eye on the water level—it should stay constant.

There is one other method of bulb forcing which I have not tried; however, it does work according to people who have used it. In this method bulbs are subjected to a cold period by themselves and not as a potted unit. Narcissus bulbs are stored at 50°F for three months and tulip bulbs at 45°F for the same length of time. Hyacinth bulbs are stored for one month at 63°F. Bulbs are then potted as usual and placed in a cool, brightly lit location such as already described in the former methods. I myself see nothing to be gained, except the ability to force more bulbs, since less cold storage area is needed. The chore of potting is not made easier, it is just postponed.

Crocus

These make an excellent bulb for forcing, since their flash of color is intense. For maximal display, put 18 corms in a six-inch pot. Sometimes it is hard to tell the bottom from the top of the corm. The bottom is slightly indented and bald; the top is covered by a hairy-looking skin. There are many species of crocus and most of them are unfamiliar to the average gardener. Most species of crocus, as well as the Dutch hybrids, force well.

Daffodil

Daffodil, which is a popular name given to the large trumpet-flowered types of the *Narcissus* genus, is a reasonably easy bulb to force. For a really spectacular display, you might try layering. Use a deep pot, as opposed to the squat bulb pan, and put in a layer of bulbs, cover them with a little soil, and place a second layer of bulbs over the spaces between the lower layer. If you use stakes, put them in before you put in the second layer of bulbs, otherwise you will probably spear a bulb at a later date. Sometimes you get a succession of bloom and other times you get one large display all at once.

When you purchase your bulbs, look for those with the double neck, which are more apt to give you multiple flower stalks. 'King Alfred,' 'Beersheba,' 'Golden Harvest,' 'Mount Hood,' 'Rembrandt,' and 'World's Favorite' force very well.

Hyacinth

Without a doubt these are the easiest bulbs to force, and in my opinion they are also the prettiest. Did you ever come into a house where hyacinths were in blossom? The spring-like fragrance is one of my favorite scents. When I smell it I know spring is not far away. It is not difficult to pick a variety for forcing; they all seem to succeed so well. Hyacinths make an ideal first choice for the beginning bulb forcer. This is one bulb where "select the biggest" can be ignored. Medium-sized bulbs are my choice, because the largest bulbs produce huge blooms which are rather top-heavy.

Hyacinths are the most aromatic of the flowering bulbs. They are also the easiest to force into bloom.

Narcissus

Of course the easiest of these is the very fragrant paper white narcissus *(N. tazetta* var. *papyraceus)* and a yellow variety called *soleil d'or.* Be careful where you buy these bulbs; they are usually cold pretreated and, as such, need no cold period to force bloom. However, I have gotten bulbs which produced abundant flowers and other batches which produced no flowers. I suspect they were not properly preconditioned. Do not save your paper whites, the preconditioning treatment and their tenderness makes them unsuitable for further use. Of the winter hardy narcissus, the miniature species *N. bulbocodium, N. minimus,* and *N. triandrus* are worth forcing. Varieties of choice include, 'February Gold,' 'Silver Chimes,' 'W.P. Milner,' 'Sir Watkins,' and 'Peeping Tom.'

Tulips

These are the more difficult Dutch bulbs when it comes to forcing. If you decide to try them, pick an early single or double variety. Remember to plant them with the flat side of the bulb toward the pot rim. The flat side is where the first large leaves appear, so placing them this way will center your blossoms. Some early varieties you might force include 'Brilliant Star,' 'White Hawk,' 'Fuga,' 'Peach Blossom,' 'General DeWett,' and 'Duc van Thol cochineal' (also scarlet and white maxima).

These are by no means all the bulbs you can force. However, they are among the easier ones. When you feel the need for new challenges, try some of the minor bulbs such as snowdrops, scilla, chiorodoxas, and grape hyacinths. One half hardy bulb, *Iris reticulata*, is also well suited for those who wish to expand their forcing horizons.

Chapter 10

From Garbage Can to House Plant

Hold it! Is that the garbage you're throwing out (or are ready to compost)? Did you know that your garbage is a special source of house plants? Although they may not be glamorous ones, these plants do provide fun, they are especially interesting to children, and they cost next to nothing. Let's pick through your garbage and see what we can find. When it is a rainy day, you may find it a good time to start your children or yourself on a garbage hunt for future house plants. Of course, some fruits and vegetables can be house plants before they are leftovers.

Avocado

After you have enjoyed your avocado, do not throw away the pit. Of course you have removed it carefully without damaging it. One point must be kept in mind. There are two market avocados; these derive from California and Florida. The larger ones come from Florida and these are more apt to succeed for the indoor gardener.

Wash the pit in lukewarm water and soak it in warm water for four or five hours. After soaking you should easily be able to remove the brown outer coating to aid the process of germination.

Now you have two methods to turn your pit into a tree. I do not know which one is better, but I personally prefer the soil method. Place the pit in a pot of all-purpose soil and cover it with one-half inch of soil. Sometimes it is difficult to recognize which part of the pit is the base; when you remove the pit, the base is usually broader and is always that part of the pit farthest from the fruit stem. The seed germinates best at 85°F, which is difficult to provide in the home without some form of bottom heat. However, they do germinate at ordinary room temperatures; they just take a little longer. Germination will require four or five weeks or even two months. If no shoots emerge after three months, your pit was a dud. You may have to try several pits, since mature ones, which are necessary for success, are not easy to recognize.

In the second method, the pit is rooted in water. Stick three toothpicks in the pit and suspend it over a glass so that the lower end is covered with water. Keep it at 70°F in a shaded place and do not let the water level drop. You will have to be patient, as this method takes as long as the first. When the roots are one-half inch long, carefully transfer the pit to a pot—do not split the pit during the process. Allow the tip of the pit to show.

Keep your plant in an east or west window and allow the top inch of soil to dry between waterings. When your plant is six inches tall, pinch out the top to encourage branching, unless, of course, you like telephone poles. Avocados, being tropical trees, require as much humidity as African violets. During the winter, you might have to resort to humidity-increasing tricks (see Chapter 1). Fertilize your avocado bi-monthly with fish emulsion. If you desire a bushy tree, just keep pinching the growing tips. Do not expect anything except handsome foliage, as the light intensity inside is insufficient for production of flowers and fruit.

Carrot

The next time you have carrots, cut off the top two inches. If there is any green foliage, trim it so that it's about one inch high. Place this top piece (foliage end up) in a bowl of wet sand or pebbles; use pebbles to help prop it up if needed. If you're using sand, keep it moist; or if you're starting it in pebbles, let the water nearly cover the carrot top. Put the bowl in a south, east, or west window. Soon leaves will begin to grow. The leaves will eventually give out and you will never be able to pick any carrots, but the lush foliage will look nice. You can grow beet and turnip greens in the same way.

You can also make a hanging basket from a carrot. Remove the leaves from a plump carrot and cut off the narrow end. Hollow out the carrot with a paring knife or apple corer, but leave enough of a shell to hold water. Attach three pieces of wires or string to the open end, hang the carrot filled with water in a window, and wait for the leaves to grow.

Citrus

Save your seeds from that grapefruit, lemon, lime, orange, or tangerine. Soak them in lukewarm water for 12 hours prior to planting. Place them pointed end up in all-purpose soil and cover them with one-quarter of an inch of soil. Keep the soil moist and place the pot in a warm (70°F), dark place. When the seeds sprout, put the pot in a southern or eastern window. After they have two or three pairs of leaves, you may wish to thin or transplant them. Allow the soil to dry out (top two or three inches) between waterings. Citrus seeds will produce dark green masses of glossy foliage. Do not expect any flowers or fruit. If you want fruit, see citrus in Chapter 11.

Coffee

To grow a coffee tree from seed, you must obtain un-roasted coffee beans. Unless you live near a business that supplies special coffee blends to restaurants or gourmet shops, these are not easy to get locally. There are some mail order houses, though, that do sell beans for planting. Park's Seed Company is one of these. Once you get your seeds, soak them in warm water overnight and then sow them in a pot of all-purpose soil. They may take 50 days to germinate or even as long as one year, depending on how long they were dormant prior to planting. Keep your coffee tree in an east window or lightly shaded southern window. Water enough so that the soil is evenly moist, but not soggy. During the summer you can put your tree outside when the evening temperature remains above 60°F. You will probably get attractive, waxy green foliage, fragrant, white star-shaped flowers, and red berries. Each berry contains two seeds and these seeds or beans are the ones which are roasted and ground for coffee.

Date Palm

Purchase unpasteurized dates, which are usually sold in health food stores, and plant several pits in a pot of all-purpose soil. Cover them with an inch of soil and keep them dark. When sprouted, put them in a southern window. You will get a palm with featherly foliage which is quite attractive, but no dates.

Grapes

Sow the seeds from your table grapes. Leave three seedlings in a five–inch pot of all-purpose soil. Put it in a southern window and train the vines around the window. It will surprise you with its aggressive growth.

Irish Potato

Take a white potato and cut off a section which has two or three "eyes" (buds). Plant it in all-purpose soil about three inches deep in a flower pot. Keep the soil evenly moist and place the pot in a southern or eastern window. Eventually you will have an attractive potato plant.

You can also grow a potato with hair. Slice off the top quarter of a white potato and hollow out an area large enough to hold a moist wad of cotton. Sprinkle the cotton thickly with seeds of lettuce, watercress, or grass. Keep it moist and watch the green hair grow on your potato head. For real authenticity, put on two buttons for eyes, a cork for a nose, and paint on a mouth. Kids really love this one.

Onion

Take a medium-sized onion and set it in a glass container, and put water in the container so that the bottom of the onion is wet. Keep it dark until roots appear and then place it in a southern or eastern window. Leaves will appear and perhaps even a flower.

Sweet Potato

You must find sweet potatoes which were not oven-dried to retard spoilage. Look in a health food store or at a small greengrocer. Select an old, firm one, preferably with sprouts. Place it in a glass jar or container of such a size that the potato will be half in and half out. Put enough water in the container to wet the bottom of the tuber, and keep it in the dark for 10 days while roots form. Do not let it dry out. Bring it to a southern or eastern window and pinch out all but three or four of the best shoots. The heart-shaped leaves on the vines are quite nice. If you want to keep it for a long time, you can pot it up in all-purpose soil. I remember this one fondly, as it was one of my first childhood plants. Sweet potatoes, which were not oven-dried, were also easier to find in those days.

Pineapple

See Chapter 8 for a discussion of this plant.

Chapter 11

The Large World
of Ornamental House Plants

In the pages to follow, you can read about many of the almost countless number of house plants. Since it would be impossible to cover all house plants, only those that are apt to find their way into your home from commercial sources or friends are discussed. Environmental needs of each plant are pointed out. However, due to variations of conditions in the home and the differing abilities of plants to tolerate adverse conditions, these are meant only as guides. Naturally some plants tolerate more abuse than others, and when known this is indicated. All in all, there is something for everybody, whether you are a novice wanting an easy plant, a moderately successful houseplant grower wishing for a challenge, or a bored-with-success grower wishing for something different.

Plants are listed in alphabetical order by their common name or names, if there are several. Common names are printed in roman type. Scientific names are indicated in italics, and when they follow the common name(s) they are in parentheses. The scientific name is often of two parts: The first word, which is capitalized, is the genus, and the second word, which is not capitalized, is the species. This scientific name may be followed by one of three things: 1. an italicized name, called a variety, which is a naturally occuring variation of the species reproducible from seed; 2. a name in roman type and single quotes which is a horticultural variety or cultivar known only in cultivation and is not necessarily reproducible from seed; or 3. a name in double quotes, which is an older scientific name no longer correct, but is still in common usage.

On the first line of each entry you will observe a code of letters and numbers. This code is an abbreviated way of expressing the cultural requirements of the plant under discussion. The first letter of the code indicates the optimum temperature range, the second letter the best humidity requirements, the middle number the soil mixture, the third letter (or fourth unit in code) the light factor, and the last letter the watering needs. The specific meaning of each code unit, as in the above sequence, is as follows:

Temperature
   C   stands for cool temperature lovers, plants that like daytime temperatures of 55° to 60°F and nighttime temperatures of 40° to 45°F.
   I   stands for intermediate temperature lovers, those plants that appreciate nighttime temperatures of 50° to 55°F and a daytime temperature of 70°F.
   W stands for plants that do best in warm temperatures, those that like a daytime high of 80° to 85°F and a nighttime low of 62° to 65°F.

Plants with a rating of I and W can be grown in most homes where there is a slight nighttime temperature drop and a daytime temperature of 68° to 70°F is maintained. Plants that like the temperature range C can be grown on a semi-heated porch or breezeway or in an area where you have created a cool microclimate. For a complete discussion of temperature parameters, please see Chapter 1.

Humidity
   A   stands for those plants which can tolerate the average home relative humidity. Ideally this should be a relative humidity of 40 to 50 percent.
   G   stands for those plants which require somewhat more humidity, such as those levels found in a greenhouse. Some of these plants will only thrive in a terrarium, but most G plants will tolerate home humidity (A) conditions. This will be indicated.

See Chapter 1 for a discussion on humidity and how to raise it when needed.

Soil

    1 stands for those plants that like the all-purpose soil.

    2 stands for those that do best in the humus lover's soil.

    3 stands for plants that require the cacti and succulent soil mixes (xerophyte formula).

    4 stands for those that like the ephiphyte formula. See Chapter 1 for the details on preparing these soil mixes.

Light

    N stands for subdued light, such as that found at a sunless north window or lightly shaded east or west window.

    M stands for moderate light, such as that in an east, west, or lightly shaded south window.

    B stands for bright, sunny daylight found only at an unshaded southern window.

Keep in mind that screens, lace or net curtains, overhanging roofs, trees, and increased distances from the window all decrease the available light. Read Chapter 1 for other considerations of light and Chapter 2 if you want to use fluorescent lights instead of natural sunlight.

Watering

    D stands for those plants that like to be drenched and then be allowed to dry their top couple of inches of soil before they are watered again.

    E stands for those plants that like their soil to be evenly moist, that is, damp and not soggy or dry.

    S stands for those plants that like their soil soaked and kept at a constant wetness.

Watering can be affected by many conditions, so reread Chapter 3 to get a better understanding of this subject. Most house plants fall into the *D* and *E* categories.

Abutilon—see Flowering maple

Acalypha hispida—see Chenille plant

Achimenes—see Magic flower

Adiantum—see Ferns

Aechmea—see Living vase plant

Aeschynanthus—see Lipstick plant

African violet *(Saintpaulia)*

W, G, 2, M, E. Undoubtedly
the queen of the gesneriad family,
these tropical African beauties are
not too difficult to grow if you heed
their cultural requirements. A minimum of effort will reward you with
almost continual blooming. Heart-
shaped leaves can be smooth, velvety, hairy, ruffled, scalloped, or
variegated. Flowers are single, semi-
double, or double in shades of blue,
pink, white, lavender, or purple.
Plants are also available in miniature
form.

African violet

When watering leaves, do not
splash them with cold water, because they will water spot. Tepid
water will not cause spots unless the
plants are watered while the sun is
shining on them. Where African violets touch pot rims in clay pots, a
condition called stem or petiole rot
occurs. This condition can be pre-
vented by dipping clay pot rims in
paraffin or using plastic pots. Insufficient humidity causes leaf curl and
bud drop. African violets are propagated most easily from leaf cuttings
and more slowly from seeds.

Since there are thousands of
African violets to choose from, it is
difficult to recommend any few in
particular. I prefer doubles over singles, because single flowers are
prone to early dropping of petals.

Aglaonema modestum—see Chinese evergreen

Air pine—see Living vase plant

Air plant—see *Kalanchoe*

Alloplectus—see Gesneriads

Aloe variegata—see Medicine plant

Aloe vera—see Medicine plant

Aluminum plant or watermelon pilea
(Pilea cadierei)

Left to right: Aluminum plant, Artillery plant, *and* Pan-American Friendship plant

W, A, 1, M, E. This southeast Asian plant is noted for its dark green quilted leaves, which appear to have aluminum stripes on them. Occasionally it has insignificant tiny flowers borne in stalked heads. Unless pinched back, it tends to get "leggy" during the winter. The aluminum plant, as well as other species of *Pilea,* are propagated from cuttings. The *Pilea* make excellent house plants. A cultivar of the aluminum plant, *Pilea cadierei* 'Minima,' is generally preferred because of its dwarf, compact (freely branching) nature.

Other interesting *Pilea* species are *Pilea involucrata* (Pan-American Friendship plant), *Pilea microphylla* (Artillery plant), *Pilea nummulariifolia* (Creeping Charlie), and *Pilea repens* (Blackleaf Panamiga). These *Pilea* originate in the tropics of our own hemisphere. *P. involucrata* has coppery-red leaves and is sometimes used in terraria, *P. micro-*

phylla is noted for its artillery-like discharge of pollen, *P. nummulariifolia* makes an excellent hanging basket plant with its small, crinkled green leaves, and *P. repens* has quilted, glossy copper-brown leaves.

There is also a very attractive *Pilea* noted especially for its unusual foliage. It appears to abound in supermarkets. Oddly enough, it is known as 'Moon Valley' and can be found in this chapter under that name.

Amaryllis *(Hippeastrum)*

I, A, 1, B, E. Amaryllis bulbs are usually imported from the Netherlands, and to a lesser degree, South America and South Africa. Dazzling shades of red, pink, orange, and white are available; purchase the bulbs in the fall. Buy a larger size, as the spectacular blossoms are worth the extra cost.

Artillery plant

December through March is the normal time to start potting these bulbs. Pick a pot large enough so that there will be only one inch of space around the widest part of the bulb: these plants bloom best when they're pot-bound. Leave one-third of the bulb above the soil line.

Once the bulb is potted you can do one of two things: either water the bulb and place it directly in a sunny southern or eastern window, or water it and keep it dark until the first growth appears. I prefer to put mine in the sun because it will blossom earlier. Do water the bulb sparingly at this stage to avoid rotting the bulb before it develops good roots.

Despite what the old tale says, it is not true that your plant will not bloom if the leaves appear before the flower stalk. This was true of older varieties, but not modern cultivars. The flower stalk (scape) is easily recognized; it is much fatter than the leaves when it emerges.

Amaryllis

Once growth appears, follow the coded cultural directions (see above). Turn your pot occasionally, since the amaryllis leans toward the sun. Although it will get tall, it requires no staking because it has such a sturdy flower stalk. After four or more weeks of rapid growth, your plant will bloom. Depending upon its age, you may find one, two, three, or four trumpet-like flowers on one stalk. Very large bulbs produce up to three flower stalks in succession.

When the flowers have faded, cut off the stalks. Do not remove any leaves, because they supply next year's blooming nourishment. Fertilize every two weeks now and put the pot outdoors during the summer. During late fall bring it indoors, stop fertilizing, and decrease water to induce dormancy. Leaves will yellow and dry. Store it in the basement and water it once a month or more if the bulb starts to shrivel.

If a bulb is not induced into dormancy, it may or may not do it on its own. Bulbs which do not go dormant still bloom, but at a much later date. Replace the top third of the soil during dormancy, and repot only when necessary. Begin the cycle again in December by watering your plant and giving it sun.

Amaryllis may be propagated either by the little offsets produced by the parent bulb or by seed. It takes about three years from offsets to blossoms, if the plants are kept at maximal growth.

Aphelandra—see Zebra plant

Aralia *(Fatsia japonica)*

C, A, 1, M, E. These Japanese evergreen shrubs have leathery, maple-like, dark shiny green leaves. The pointed lobes are toothed. Quite tolerant, they are good plants for difficult areas. Prune them severely in the spring since they are apt to get tall and lanky. Propagate from seeds or spring cuttings. The best for the house is *F. japonica* 'Moseri.' A variegated form, *F. japonica variegata,* is very attractive.

Aralia ivy—see Tree ivy

Araucaria excelsa—see Norfolk Island pine

Ardisia crenata—see Coral berry

Ariocarpus—see Cacti

Artillery plant—see Aluminum plant

Asparagus fern, Emerald feather *(Asparagus)*

I, A, 1, M, E. Both of these plants—asparagus fern *(Asparagus plumosus)* and emerald feather *(Asparagus sprengeri)*—come from South Africa. They are not too difficult to grow as house plants. Of the two, *A. sprengeri* is the better house plant. It has flat needle-like, feather cascades of foliage which look spectacular in a hanging basket. If possible, keep it on the cooler side in the winter. Tiny white flowers appear, which become bright red berries some times around Christmas. *Asparagus plumosus* tends to be a tall climber with very fine lacey, fern-like leaves. It has purple black berries. Another variety, *A. meyeri,* is interesting, with its dense, upright plumes of needle-like foliage. They are all easily propagated from seed or by division.

Asparagus fern *(Asparagus plumosus)*

Asparagus plumosus—see Asparagus fern

Asparagus sprengeri—see Asparagus fern

Aspidistra elatior—see Cast-iron plant

Asplenium—see Ferns

Astrophytum—see Cacti

Avocado—see Chapter 10

Baby's tears *(Helxine soleirollii)*

I, G, , M, E. This plant, native to Sardinia and Corsica, is a low, moss-like creeper with numerous, tiny, round bright green leaves.

Baby's tears will cascade
over a pot rim, or make an
excellent ground cover in a
pot with other plants or in
a terrarium. As long as the
humidity is around 50 percent or more, it will thrive.
I favor it as a ground cover
in a terrarium or bottle garden. A cultivar, 'Aurea,' is
quite unusual with its ivory to deep
yellow-colored leaves.

Baby's tears

Banana—see Chapter 8

Begonia

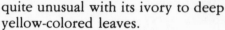

W, A, (some G), 2, M, D. A
person could spend the rest of his or
her life growing these as house
plants. Once only unknown natives
of the warmer regions, such as the
forests of Central and South America, now there are at least 6000
named species and varieties of begonias. In general they can be
propagated from seed or leaf and
stem cuttings, or in some species, by
division of tubers and rhizomes. Begonias are noted for their handsome
foliage and beautiful flowers. Keeping them slightly pot-bound promotes blooming; some pruning is
required to promote branching and
to keep them in shape. Begonias are
grouped according to their root systems: rhizomatous, tuberous, and
fibrous.

Tuberous types, which are dormant in the winter and bloom in the
summer on a porch or patio, are not
suitable house plants. Bulbous

types, which are included under the tuberous varieties, like cool nights and high humidity and are best left to the florist.

Many of the rhizomatous begonias are too large to be good house plants, although some of the dwarfs are quite charming. Some rest slightly during the winter; you should decrease their water at that time. Rex begonias are included in this group too; they are fussy about humidity and can be troublesome under house conditions. Most rex begonias undergo a dormant period during the winter. You might try some of the popular rhizomatous begonias such as the beefsteak begonias, *B. erythrophylla* and *B. erythrophylla bunchii;* the star begonias, *B. ricinifolia, B. sunderbruchii,* "Joe Hayden" (good for beginners); the dwarf begonias, *B. boweri* (eyelash begonia), *B. rotundifolia,* and *B. hydrocotylifolia;* and the rex begonias, 'Helen Lewis' (good for beginners), 'Baby Rainbow,' 'Calico,' and 'King Edward.' Flowers are usually pink, white, or red.

The fibrous group is the largest and they make the best house plants. Subgroups such as wax begonias *(B. semperflorens),* angel wing or cane-stemmed types, small-leaved branching kinds, and the hairy or hirsute begonias make this a colorful group.

The wax begonias *(B. semperflorens)* make excellent, reasonably carefree house plants with their waxy green or reddish leaves and

Begonia

single or double flowers in shades of
white, pink, or red. They bloom
happily indoors all winter and continue blooming outdoors in the
summer. They are ideal for borders.
A variety of *B. semperflorens,* Calla
begonia, has green leaves with
white mottlings. Any variety you
choose is good. They are quite easy
to grow from seed.

The angel wing types, characterized by their colorful wing-
shaped leaves, are beautiful, but
tend to get very large. They should
be kept a little moister than other
begonias. Some good varieties are
'Alzasco,' 'Orange-Rubra,' 'Pink-
Rubra,' and 'Corallina De Lucerna'
(good for beginners).

For attractive begonias, try
'Preussen' and 'Sachsen,' two small-
leaved branching types. Some good
hairy begonias (hairy or shiny leathery leaves, fast growers, tolerant of
low humidity) are *B. scharffii,* an
old-time favorite, *B. alleryi, B. pruni-
folia, B. drostii,* and *B. viaudi.*

There are many more varieties
of begonias and much more which
could be said about these colorful
plants. But then, that is why there
are books that cover just this one
plant.

Bellonia—see Gesneriads

Beloperone guttata—see Shrimp plant

Billbergia—see Pitcher plant

Bird of paradise *(Strelitzia reginae)*

I, A, 1, B, D. This South African plant has banana-like leaves and

an orange-yellow, bird-shaped flower that has a blue "tongue." The flowers, borne on a spike, appear in spring and early summer. In order to bloom, they must have seven to 10 leaves and under most cases, spend the summer outdoors on a porch, a patio, or in light shade. Propagation is by division or suckers. It is a fairly tough plant.

Bird's nest fern—see Ferns

Blackleaf Panamiga—see Aluminum plant

Blechnum—see Ferns

Boea—see Gesneriads

Boxwood *(Buxus microphylla japonica)*

C, A, 1, B, E. This Japanese evergreen shrub, which has glossy, bright green, leathery leaves, is sometimes grown as a house plant. It is ideal in cool, sunny situations and could be a possibility for bonsai because of its slow growth. Propagate it by hardwood cuttings in the autumn, or by division.

Brake fern—see Ferns

Briggsia—see Gesneriads

Bromeliads *(Bromeliaceae)*

W, A, 4, M, E (in general). There are approximately 1800 species in the bromeliad family. Most bromeliads are noted for their magnificently marked leaves, which grow in a rosette. They are equally known for their flower spikes of bracts and flowers in such beautiful color combinations as rose and blue. These flowers often last for a long time and are sometimes followed by colored berries.

Bromeliads, natives of the Central and South American tropics, are mostly epiphytes (or tree crotch dwellers), although some are ground dwellers. Their root systems function mainly to support them in the organic matter in the tree crotch; water and nutrients are usually obtained through the rosette leaves, which form a type of water "cup." At home keep this cup filled with water and change it every two weeks; add a weak solution of fish emulsion directly to the water cup once a month during the growing season, but probably not at all during the winter. During the summer and spring, keep the soil moist, but keep it on the drier side in the winter.

If flowers fail to appear, you can force them by enclosing the plant and a ripe apple within a sealed plastic bag for several days. The ethylene gas, which is released from the apple, will initiate blossoming.

Propagation is usually by suckers, offshoots, and division. This is best done during the spring or early summer.

There are many species, and some of the best are listed in this chapter under the following headings which you should see:

> Living vase plant or air pine
> *(Aechmea)*
>
> Pineapple *(Ananas)*—see Chapter 8
>
> Pitcher plant *(Billbergia)*
>
> Earth stars *(Cryptanthus)*
>
> *Greigia sphacelata*
>
> *Neoregelia*
>
> *Tillandsia*
>
> *Vriesia*

Bryophyllum—see *Kalanchoe*

Bulbs (forcing)—see Chapter 9

Burn plant—see Medicine plant

Butterfly palm—see Palms

Butterwort—see Meat-eating plants

Button fern—see Ferns

Buxus microphylla japonica—see Boxwood

Cacti *(Cactaceae)*

Various cacti

W or I, A, 3, B, D—all year 'round (xerophytes or desert dwellers); W, A, 4, M, E—spring and summer; C, A, 4, M, D—autumn, winter (epiphytes or tree crotch dwellers).

Cacti make excellent house plants because they have built-in tolerance—Nature designed them to succeed under adverse environmental conditions. Requiring a minimum of care and offering a choice of over 2000 species, it is no wonder that some people make cacti their lifetime hobby.

About the only major cause of failure is overwatering, especially during the winter. During that season, watering once a week or every two weeks is sufficient. If they need more water you will know by the shriveling of the tissue as the stored water is utilized.

Various cacti can be propagated from seed, (a very slow process), offsets, or cuttings (allow to air dry and form a callus before rooting to prevent rotting). Wear gloves or use forceps when handling cacti, because some of those spines and minute fibrous needles can do a job on your hands.

Strangely enough cacti can be found both in the desert and in the jungle. We are familiar with desert cacti (xerophytes) and most of us know a jungle cactus, the Christmas cactus. During part of the year jungle cacti (epiphytes or tree crotch dwellers) receive much rain but they are also subjected to a dry period.

A description of some of the cacti genera follows. Unless specified otherwise, they are xerophytes. Most of them, if given enough sun and cool temperatures (55°F) in the winter, will bloom.

Ariocarpus (living rock cactus) —Nearly spineless, the globular Mexican cacti have triangular scales in a spiral pattern. Most of the plant grows below ground.

Astrophytum (Star cactus)—These Mexican cacti are a refreshing change from the pincushion-and barrel-type cacti, with their prominent thorns and deeply indented trunks.

Cephalocereus—These are barrel-shaped Mexican cacti with a covering of long white "hair." *C. senilis* is known as the old man cactus for obvious reasons.

Echinocactus (barrel cactus)—Their appearance is suggestive of a thorny barrel or cylinder.

Echinocereus (hedgehog cactus)—These are usually low-growing globes or cylinders, deeply ribbed and spiny.

Hedgehog cactus

Echinopsis (Easter lily cactus)—Very similar to *Echinocereus.*

Epiphyllum—These epiphytes, known as orchid cacti, are very large and quite droopy. They need support or room to droop.

Gymnocalycium (barrel cactus)—Globular shapes and easy flowering are characteristic of these Argentinean cacti.

Hylocereus—An epiphyte, which is often called night blooming cereus, is noted for its night white flowers which last one night. If you have a lot of room and patience, you might like it.

Mammillaria—This is often called pincushion cactus because of its resemblance to one.

Notocactus (ball cactus)—These cylindrical or globular cacti from South America flower freely.

Opuntia—These native American cacti vary in shape from flat with ear-like branches, to cylindrical. Some of them are known as prickly pear and bunny ears. The smaller ones make excellent house plants.

Pereskia (lemon vine)—These vine-like cacti from Mexico have spines, lemon-scented flowers, and narrow leaves. They are refreshing changes from the usual cacti.

Rebutia (crown cactus)—These small, barrel-shaped cacti from Argentina are more reliable than most other cacti when it comes to annual spring blossoms.

Two cacti grafted together

Rhipsalis—This epiphyte, sometimes called chain or mistletoe cactus, has long hanging strands of jointed segments. Blooming reluctantly, but growing slowly, they make an interesting hanging basket plant.

Schlumbergera—See Holiday cacti.

Selenicereus—This is another epiphyte, called night blooming cereus, which is found in South American jungles. Requiring much room, they have little to recommend themselves.

Zygocactus—See Holiday cacti.

Caladium

W, G, 2, M, E. These tropical South American plants are grown from tubers. Leaves are spectacular with their splashes of green, cream, pink, red, and white; shapes vary from heart-shaped to long arrow-shaped. Not overly unreasonable in their demands, these plants are worth a try. Propagate by division of tubers.

Caladium

Start tubers in late winter for spring color or in spring for summer color. They are ideal plants for the summer porch or patio. Bury the tubers in a mixture of compost and sand (one-half inch deep) and keep the bottom warm (80°F) by placing the container over a wet pebble tray on a radiator or by using a heating cable. When they start to root, pot them up—they should be buried two inches deep. After the leaves fade, withhold water and store the dry tubers in a plastic bag at 60°F for two months. There are at least 50 beautiful cultivars from which to choose.

Calamondin orange—See *Citrus*

Calathea makoyana—See Peacock plant

Calliandra inaequilatera—See Powder-puff plant

Camellia japonica—See Common camellia

Cape Primrose *(Streptocarpus)*

I, G, 2, M, E. These African plants, which are members of the gesneriad family, vary extensively in their characteristics. In general they are no more difficult to grow than African violets. Leaves are rather long, quilted, and ungainly. Flowers are open-faced funnels in hues of violet, blue, white, pink, and crimson; they are the focal point of this plant. Plants can be everblooming, although some show a tendency to go dormant, and some even die after setting seed. If they show signs of dormancy, reduce watering and move to a cooler place. Resume normal culture at first signs of new growths. Propagation is from pieces of mature leaf attached to the leaf stalk. The Rexii hybrids are the best for growing ease.

Capsicum annuum conoides—see Christmas pepper

Carissa grandiflora—see Natal plum

Caryota—see Palms

Cast-iron plant *(Aspidistra elatior)*

I, A, 1, N, E. This member of the lily family is a native of China. As the name implies, it is a tough plant which succeeds under adverse conditions. It is now regaining the popularity it enjoyed during Victorian times.

The long, wide leaves arch in a graceful fashion. Flowers are purple-brown bells borne near the soil line. They are pollinated by snails in their native habitat, but indoors, propagation is through rootstock division. Plants can remain in the same pot for three or four years.

Cast-iron plant

A variegated form, *A. elatior* 'Variegata,' is quite attractive with its green and white striped leaves. A dwarf, *A. elatior* 'Minor,' is also available. If you are looking for a Victorian antique, this plant is for you!

Cattleya—see Orchids

Cephalocereus—see Cacti

Ceropegia woodii—see String of hearts

Chain fern—see Ferns

Chamaedorea—see Palms

Chenille plant *(Acalypha hispida)*

W, G, 1, M, E. This showy tropical shrub comes from India. Leaves are broad, bright green ovals with rounded, toothed edges and a hairy appearance. Flowers are bright red, long pendant spikes which resemble foxtails. Prune this in the spring; you can root spring or fall cuttings if you supply bottom heat. Rather fussy about humidity, this plant may give you trouble. A variety, *alba*, has creamy white flower spikes which are tinted slightly pink.

Chinese banyan—see *Ficus*

Chinese Evergreen *(Aglaonema modestum)*

W, A, 1, N, E. This southeast Asian plant is quite a tolerant individual, capable of surviving even in hot, dry, dim apartments. It has waxy leaves and grows rather slowly. If pot-bound, flowers borne on a spathe with leaf petioles encircling the stem may appear (similar to Jack-in-the pulpit). Propagation is by rootstock division or cuttings.

There are some rather interesting cultivars, such as *A. modestum* 'Variegatum' (a creamy variegated form), *A. commutatum* (silver gray leaf markings), *A. pictum* (dainty, silver gray leaf patches), *A. simplex* (leaves thinner and more papery than *A. modestum,* with which it is often confused), and 'Fransher' (a colorful cultivar with leaves milky green to green variegated with cream).

Chirita—see Gesneriads

Chlorophytum comosum 'Vittatum'—see Spider plant

Christmas cactus—see Holiday cacti

Christmas pepper (*Capsicum annuum conoides* [*'frutescens'*])

W, A, 1, B, E. These are also known as bird peppers or ornamental peppers and are closely related to the garden pepper. They have green pointed oval leaves and small conical peppers which turn bright red.

The best of these is Red Chile, which has edible sweet-spicy red peppers that remain on the plant at Christmastime. Since these are easy annuals, start them from seed around May and keep them potted outdoors during the summer. Bring them inside in the fall. Although they only last a year, they are worth growing for their cheery winter color and edible peppers.

Chrysalidocarpus—see Palms

Chrysothemis—see Gesneriads

Cissus—see Grape ivy

Citrus

I, A, 1, B, D. These tropical plants, which include oranges, lemons, and limes, have species suited to home environments. Being both ornamental and edible, they are very practical house plants. Leaves are pointed ovals of deep green. The waxy, white flowers fill the whole house with their very pleasant fragrance. Often a plant will have flowers and both ripe and unripe fruit at the same time. Flowers appear in late winter and may last to the summer, if you put the plant outdoors after all danger of frost is past. Hand pollination with a soft paintbrush will improve fruit setting. Occasional pruning will keep them shapely. Since citrus does best in a slightly acid soil, it does not hurt to water them once a month with a half teaspoon of vinegar diluted in one quart of water. Propagate from cuttings of half-ripened wood. The better species for house culture are detailed below.

Lemon—The best known for indoor use are Ponderosa lemon (*C. limon* 'Ponderosa') and Meyer lemon (*C. limon* 'Meyeri'). The Ponderosa or American wonder lemon grows very stout spines and

Ponderosa lemon

bears pear-shaped yellow fruit weighing as much as three pounds. While very sour, the fruit is edible. The Meyer lemon tree is less spiny and produces small fruit of good quality. If your room is limited, it is the better of the two.

Lime—*Citrus aurantifolia* or lime does not seem to have many varieties useful for home culture. You might try the key lime from Florida, or 'Bearss', a variety of the Tahiti or Persian lime group.

Orange—Good varieties include Calamondin orange *(C. mitis)*, Otaheite orange *(C. taitensis)*, and Myrtleleaf orange *(C. aurantium myrtifolia)*. All are nearly spineless trees. The fruits are small, orange, and quite sour. They are best used

Calamondin orange

as substitutes for lemon juice or for use in marmalades.

All of the above, with suitable training, can make interesting bonsai.

Clerodendrum—see Glorybower

Clivia—see Kafir lily

Club moss *(Selaginella kraussiana)*

W, G, 2, N, E. Relatives of ferns, these are ideal terrarium plants. Some are small creepers, others are erect, and still others are climbers. They are found in tropical regions. Propagate from cuttings. The toughest is probably *S. kraussiana,* a small creeper. *S. emmeliana* is usually available and is erect and fern-like. *S. willdenovii* is a climber with startling blue leaves.

Club moss

Cobra plant—see Meat-eating plants

Codiaeum variegatum pictum—see Croton

Codonanthe—see Gesneriads

Coffea arabica—see Coffee tree

Coffee tree *(Coffea arabica)*

W, A, 1, M, E. This evergreen shrub originally came from Ethiopia and Angola. Leaves are large, shiny and dark green; flowers are white and fragrant. Red berries which follow the flowers each contain two coffee beans. They can be propagated from cuttings or unroasted coffee beans. Of medium difficulty to grow and main-

Coffee tree

tain, they make an attractive accent plant. Don't expect to get many coffee beans to roast and grind from your tree.

Coleus *(Coleus blumei)*

W, A, 1, B, D. Everyone is familiar with these old-fashioned foliage plants sporting brilliant hues of purple, red, pink, green, and yellow on velvety leaves. Strong sun or flourescent lights is really needed to bring out the colors. So many cultivars exist, each prettier than the next, that you can pick any and be satisfied. Since they are easy to grow from seed, you can start a mixture and put the extras or boring ones in your garden. If you grow fond of any particular ones you can propagate them from stem tip cuttings. They have spikes of blue flowers, but I pinch them off because they sap strength from the more dramatic leaves. Indoors, during the winter, they require ruthless pruning to prevent them from getting leggy.

Coleus

Coleus blumei—see Coleus

Colocasia—see Elephant ears

Columnea—see Goldfish plant

Common camellia *(Camellia japonica)*

C, A, 2, M, S. These are ornamental evergreens native to the mountains of Japan and Korea. Often they are seen outdoors in the

South. As a house plant, they are difficult to grow unless you have an unheated sunporch, breezeway, or a large, cool, bay window. Branches are woody, and the glossy green leaves have finely-toothed margins. Flowers can be waxy white or pink, singles or doubles. They usually bloom from October through January. Propagation should be from winter cuttings and pruning is best done in the early spring. Keep the soil slightly acid. Suggested cultivars for indoor culture include 'Alba plena,' 'Donkelaari,' 'Sarah Frost,' 'Pink Perfection,' and 'Debutante.'

Common fig—see Chapter 8

Common ginger *(Zingiber officinale)*

W, G, 1, B, E. Ginger is found growing in the area extending from India to the Pacific Islands. It has slender, reed-like stems and glossy, dark green, almost grass-like leaves. Ginger used for cooking comes from the tuberous rhizome of this plant, usually available in Oriental food stores. You can grow a ginger plant from this rhizome, or propagate established plants by division. The flowers are attractively borne as a cone-like cluster on a spike which has green bracts and purple-lipped, yellow marked flowers. Ginger sometimes shows signs of resting during the winter. At such times of dormancy you should decrease the frequency of waterings. If you have a sunny window, this interesting plant should do well for you.

Conandron—see Gesneriads

Coral berry *(Ardisia crenata)*

I, A, 1, M, E. Popular at Christmas because of their persistent red berries, these make fairly tolerant house plants. This species comes from China and Malaya. Leaves are thick, leathery, shiny, and dark green with crisped margins; they resemble holly. Flowers are white or reddish. As they age, they lose their lower leaves and nice appearance. Propagate from seeds or cuttings of half-ripe wood taken in the spring. There are other species, but this is probably the best for indoors.

Coral berry

Cordyline terminalis var. 'Ti'—see Ti plant

Crab cactus—see Holiday cacti

Crassula

I, A, 3, B, D. These African succulents make good house plants because of their high tolerance level. While some require much sun (B), others can withstand less (M, see code explanation at start of chapter). *Crassula* are characterized by their fleshy leaves and stems; leaves vary in color from gray to blue to green. Some species branch freely, while others form low rosettes of leaves. It is usually the gray-or blue-leaf plants which require more sun. Do not overwater during the winter, as spindly growth and root rot can result; once a week or even every two weeks is enough during this time. Refer also to succulents for additional information. Some of the better species follow:

Jade plant *(C. argentea)*—A freely branching succulent with thick rubbery leaves, this makes an excellent house plant that can grow quite large. It has puffs of dainty pinkish-white, star-like flowers. Leaves are glossy jade green and rounded on top; they are red underneath and turn red on the upper surface edges when there is sufficient sun. When mature, the trunk and stems develop a woody look, giving this plant an attractive, tree-like look. A smaller version, *C. argentea minima,* exists, as well as 'Dwarf Ruby' and 'Sunset,' two cultures. The latter has yellow in its leaves.

Jade plant

Necklace vine *(C. perfossa)*—This plant resembles a necklace of triangular thick leaves which are spaced closely together and trail as a vine.

Princess Pine *(C. pseudolycopodioides)*—Resembling club moss, this has close-spaced, scaly leaves borne in four ranks. Its lax, rambling manner

Necklace vine

of branching makes it an interesting plant.

C. pyramidalis—This has tricornered leaves arranged in four ranks close above each other, like a pyramid.

Creeping Charlie—see Aluminum plant

Creeping fig—see *Ficus*

Crossandra infundibuliformis—see Firecracker plant

Croton *(Codiaeum variegatum pictum)*

Princess pine

W, G, 1, B, E. These plants, which come from many tropical regions, are noted for their multicolored, highly ornamental foliage. Many interesting cultivars exist. Leaves are generally large and their shape may be oval, elliptical, thin and narrow, or lobed like an oak leaf; some forms have twisted or curled foliage. Colors found in the leaves include red, pink, yellow, cream, and green. Propagation is by stem or leaf cuttings or air layering. This is a moderately difficult plant and it tends to get leggy, but it is certainly worth the effort. Be careful, the white sap is an irritant.

Crown of thorns—see *Euphorbia*

Cryptanthus—see Earth stars

Croton

Cyclamen

C, G, 2, M, E. Found from Greece to Syria, these plants are beautiful with their succulent, heart-shaped, bluish leaves touched with silvery designs. They have large elegant, nodding flowers in hues of white, salmon, rose, and red. The florist's cyclamen, *C. persicum giganteum,* is normally available with its many colorful cultivars. This is not a good plant for the house, unless you can supply cool, humid conditions. In warm dry houses, most florists' cyclamens produce yellow leaves and withered buds. If you provide the proper conditions, it will stop blooming around April. Reduce the water and store the plant in a cool, dry place until late summer. At that time repot it and start watering. Do not get water in the crown of the tuber; if you do it will rot. It is usually propagated from seeds.

Cyperus alternifolius—see Umbrella plant

Cypripedium—see Orchids

Cyanotis somaliensis—see Pussy ears

Darlingtonia—see Meat-eating plants

Date palm—see Chapter 10

Davallia—see Ferns

Devil's backbone *(Pedilanthus tithymaloides)*

S, G, 3, M, E. This tropical American plant, sometimes known as the Redbird cactus, is frequently seen outdoors in the South. Of particular interest is its fleshy, zig zag stem ("backbone"), which has two rows of alternate glossy or waxy leaves. It can be propagated from cuttings, which must dry overnight or form a callus at the cutting point before being rooted. The white sap is a caustic irritant, so handle with care. The variety *nanus* has leathery black-green leaves, while *variegatus* has green, white, and red coloration which makes it quite attractive. Flowers are borne in red and yellow bracts. During the winter you should decrease your waterings to once a week. Of medium difficulty, it is well worth growing.

Diastema—see Gesneriads

Dieffenbachia—see Dumbcane

Dionaea—see Meat-eating plants

Dizygotheca elegantissima—see False aralia

Dracaena

W, A, 1, M, S. These tropical plants from various world regions are noted for their decorative foliage. Many species exist, so there are many forms to choose from. Generally they grow large, have a distinct stalk, and narrow, sword-like leaves. Quite tolerant, they can even succeed in apartments. As they age they tend to get stalky and should be propagated by air layering and stem cuttings.

Left: *Dracaena godseffiana*; right: *Dracaena sanderiana*

Some species you might try are *D. deremensis* 'Warnecki' (green and white variegations), *D. fragrans* (corn-like leaves, rapid grower), *D. fragrans massangeana* (a good house plant, green and yellow striped leaves), *D. marginata* (red edged leaves, slow and durable), *D. san-*

deriana (broad white marginal bands, very durable), and *D. god-seffiana* (smallest, green leaves spotted with yellow or white).

Drosera—see Meat-eating plants

Dumbcane *(Dieffenbachia)*

Dumbcane

W, A, 1, M, D. Chewing on any part of this plant will produce swelling and irritation of the mouth and tongue (origin of common name) and can result in death if swelling of the base of the tongue is sufficient to block the throat air passage. This South American tropical plant is noted for its large leaves speckled or striped in green and white and yellow. It is a rather tolerant plant which can survive under adverse conditions. Do not overwater though, as it is susceptible to root and cane rot.

As the plant ages, it tends to develop a long stalk with a crown of leaves. At this stage it should be propagated by air layering the crown to yield a new handsome plant. The leftover stalk can be cut into pieces and propagated like stem cuttings.

There are many species; *D. amoena, D. bowmannii, D.* 'Exotica,' *D. picta 'Superba,'* and *D. seguina* are all good choices.

Earth stars *(Cryptanthus)*

W, A, 4, M, D. These bromeliads are found on the ground rather than in tree crotches. They have low, sprawling, banded or striped leaf rosettes which resemble stars; small white clusters of flowers appear low in the center and are barely visible. Earth stars are usually propagated by division.

Some good species are *C. zonatus, C. bivittatus, C. beuckeri,* and *C. bromeloides tricolor* (rainbow star). More information can be found under bromeliads.

Easter cactus—see Holiday cacti

Echeveria

I, A, 3, B, D. These Mexican succulents are good house plants, as long as sufficient light is available. Fleshy leaves are arranged in blue-gray or gray-green rosettes, which are low growing and compact. Some are waxy in appearance, others appear to be felt-covered, and some have red coloration on leaf edges. If light is insufficient, they lose their color and get "leggy." Flowers are red or orange tubules, which appear in the spring or summer. Propagate from cuttings, offsets, or a single leaf. Allow them to form a callus for 24 hours before putting them in the rooting medium. A single leaf just laid on sand will root and produce a plant. (See succulents for more information.)

Echeveria

Echinocactus, Echinocereus, Echinopsis—see Cacti

Elephant ears *(Colocasia)*

W, G, 1, M, S. These tropical plants are noted for their large, heart-shaped, velvety green leaves on tall stems. Keep these plants slightly drier in the winter and propagate them from the tubers. Two good varieties are *C. antiquorum illustris* (purple markings on leaf) and *C. esculenta.* Watch the humidity with these, since they are somewhat fussy.

Emerald feather—see Asparagus fern

Epidendrum—see Orchids

Epiphyllum—see Cacti

Episcia—see Flame violets

Euonymus japonicus

C, A, 1, M, E. This is an upright evergreen shrub which comes from Japan. Not too difficult to grow, it is quite attractive with its glossy, usually variegated foliage. *E. japonicus aureo variegatus* ('Yellow Queen') has green and yellow leaves, and *E. japonicus argenteo variegatus* ('Silver Queen') has green and white leaves. A smaller dwarf form, *E. japonicus microphylla variegatus,* has green and white leaves. If temperatures are too high, it may get spindly; prune it if it does. Propagate from cuttings.

Euonymus japonicus ('Yellow queen')

Euphorbia

W, or I, A, 3, B, D. These succulents come mostly from South Africa and are the equivalent of our American cacti. Unlike our cacti though, their flowers are small and insignificant. Some are spiny and resemble cacti, while others have strange, exotic, tortured shapes.

The genus is quite diverse and has about 2000 species, among which is the poinsettia. All have a milky sap, which contains a powerful irritant that varies in potency from plant to plant. For example, a poinsettia leaf can kill a child, while one *Euphorbia* species is nontoxic enough for cattle fodder. Be leary with children and do not get the sap in cuts or your eyes.

During the winter, keep these plants on the dry side by only watering once a week or twice a month. (Also see succulents.) Propagation is by offsets (if produced) or cuttings; allow them to dry or form a callus before inserting them in the rooting medium. Seeds are difficult to obtain.

Naturally, it is impossible to cover all of the species. I will discuss a few of my favorites:

Crown of thorns *(E. splendens prostrata)*—This freely branching plant has long sharp spines and small oval leaves. It is the only *Euphorbia* that doesn't have insignificant flowers. Its red flowers are lovely. A better variety is *E. splendens bojeri,* which is smaller and less temperamental about dropping leaves.

Milk bush *(E. tirucallii)*—This spineless, branching *Euphorbia* has pencil-like green branches loaded with "milky poison." Leaves are tiny and deciduous. It does quite well in the house.

Poinsettia *(E. pulcherrima)*— We all know this popular Christmas plant with its red, pink, or white bracts and large leaves. If you get one for the holidays, slowly decrease the watering to near dryness when the leaves start to fall. Move it to a north or west cellar window or other cool area (55°F) and water it monthly. Around spring, cut it down to stand about six inches, increase watering, and put it in an east or south window. When the danger of frost is past, put it outdoors. When you bring your other house plants indoors, bring it in also, and then treat it like the cultural code above indicates. Since it is a short-day plant, it must have 14 hours of darkness to set buds. Put it in an unused room or place it in a closet every night. You should be rewarded nicely for your efforts.

Poinsettia

False Aralia *(Dizygotheca elegantissima)*

W, A, 1, M, E. These graceful shrubs, grown for their delicate foliage, come from the New Hebrides in the South Pacific. They have feathery leaves composed of long, narrow, toothed leaflets that have a leathery texture. Foliage appears metallic with a reddish brown color. It is best to buy these young, as older plants experience difficulty in adjusting to homes. Propagate them

False aralia

from cuttings. Somewhat fussy, they lose their lower leaves if humidity or light is insufficient.

Fatshedera lizei—see Tree ivy

Fatsia japonica—see Aralia

Ferns

Since the many species of ferns vary in their cultural requirements, the cultural code will be listed with those species described below. Ferns are one of our oldest plants; they followed the algae and mosses in the early days of plant evolution. Today they are grown for their beautiful form which is created by their graceful fronds. Ferns do not have flowers or seeds, but rely upon spores for reproduction. Spores, sometimes mistaken for scale, appear as brown raised dots or lines on the undersides or margins of fronds. Small ferns suitable for house plants can be grown from these in about two years, but propagating from spores is an involved process, so it's best to buy plants. Some ferns, however, may be propagated by division of plants, rootstocks, or rhizomes or from runners.

Ferns generally like warmth, high humidity, good indirect light, a humusy soil, and constant moisture. From November through February, ferns rest and will require a slight reduction in water. Many look good in hanging baskets, while others are more upright in form. Some fare better in the home than others, and these will be pointed out below.

Bird's nest fern *(Asplenium nidus)*—I, G, 2, N, S. This fern derives from the Asian and Polynesian areas. Although not as easy to grow as some ferns, it is also not the hardest. In appearance it is quite distinct from the normal fern stereotype; it has chartreuse leaf-shaped fronds (not lacy and feathery like most ferns) that spring from a fibrous bird's nest-like affair. If new plants appear around the base, they can be cut and potted.

Boston fern, 'Fluffy Ruffles' fern (varieties of *Nephrolepis exaltata*)—I, A, 1, M, E. An old-time favorite, the Boston fern *(Nephrolepis exaltata bostoniensis)* is a good choice for the house with its large, wide, pinnate green fronds. A more compact form, *N. exaltata bostoniensis compacta,* is available for those with less room. 'Fluffy Ruffles' is a dwarf cultivar of *N. exaltata* which has 12-inch long fronds. It does well in the home. The species, *N. exaltata* is found in many parts of the world. Propagation is by division of the plant or runners.

Boston fern

Brake fern (*Pteris multifida* [serrulata])—I, A, 2, N, E. This Chinese and Japanese fern is another good choice for the home. The following cultivars are especially nice: 'Cristata,' 'Cristata compacta,' and 'Voluta.' These are coarser in appearance than some of the more delicate species.

Button fern *(Pellaea rotundifolia)*—I, G, 2, N, E. A little fussy, this New Zealand fern is small and low-growing with button-like leaves. It is quite at home in a terrarium. Propagation is by rhizome division.

Chain fern *(Woodwardia orientalis)*—I, A, 1, M, E. This decorative oriental fern has large, broad fronds which are stiff and leathery. Somewhat difficult to grow, it is a challenging plant when young, but may challenge you right out of your home when older, since it gets very large. Plantlets may be produced and these can be potted.

Hare's foot fern *(Polypodium aureum)*—I, A, 2, M, E. This tropical American fern is another good choice for the home. Its creeping rhizomes scaled in rusty-brown look like rabbit feet. The blue-green fronds are large and deeply cut. The cultivars, 'Mandaianum' and 'Undulatum,' are small and attractive. Propagation is by rhizome division.

'Fluffy Ruffles' fern

Hart's tongue fern *(Phyllitis scolopendrium)*—C, G, 2, N, E. This native fern is not a good choice, unless you can supply the necessary cool temperatures. It has long straight or curved strap-like leathery fronds. Propagation is by rhizome division.

Maiden hair fern *(Adiantum)*—W, G, 2, N, S. These beautiful tropical ferns are noted for their delicate feathery foliage. If your humidity is low, they will give you trouble. However, their beauty is worth the effort that may be necessary to provide the high humidity. The most reliable is *A. cuneatum. A. caudatum* is a trailing variety. Propagate by division.

Rabbit foot fern *(Davallia fejeensis)*—I, A, 2, N, E. This tropical Pacific area fern has brown wooly rhizomes and finely cut fronds. It is a good choice for the home. A more finely cut variety, *D. fegeensis plumosa*, has a fuller appearance. Propagation is by rhizome division.

Staghorn fern *(Platycerium bifurcatum)*—I, G, (osmunda fiber) M, E. Coming from New Guinea and surrounding areas, these ferns resemble stag horns. They can be grown in a

Staghorn fern

house with moderate difficulty. Staghorn ferns are usually grown in Osmunda fiber wired to a cork or cedar slab which is often mounted on a wall or over a doorway. This fiber must be kept wet.

Tree fern *(Blechnum)*—W, G, 2, N, S. These stiff, tree-like ferns can give you trouble. If you wish to try one, *B. gibbum* is a good choice. It comes from New Caledonia.

Ficus

W, A, 1, M, E. This genus comprises a large group of plants found in many areas of Asia, Central America, Australia, Africa, and the Meditteranean region. Not only is the genus widespread, but there is a diversity of foliage and growth patterns among the species in it. Some are erect and treelike, others are trailers; leaves vary from large and leathery to small in form. Generally the various species of *Ficus* are tolerant and make excellent house plants. Usually the tree forms are propagated by air layering and the smaller types by division. A very few of the more popular species are described below:

Chinese Banyan *(F. retusa)*— This is a tree form covered with dense foliage. As the tree ages, the branches become pendulous. Leaves are small, leathery, and waxy. A variety, *F. retusa nitida,* is called Indian laurel and is somewhat reminiscent of mountain laurel.

Common fig *(F. carica)*—see Chapter 8.

Creeping fig (*F. pumila* [*"repens"*])—This is a freely branching creeper with small (one-inch), dark green leaves. It has hold-fast roots like ivy and can be trained on cedar bark. A smaller, slower-growing variety, *F. pumila minima,* is rather interesting, and a variegated variety (*F. pumila* 'Variegata'), is quite attractive.

Creeping fig

Fiddle-leaf fig (*F. lyrata* [pandurata])—This is another tree type and is even more tolerant as a house plant than most *Ficus.* It has large, dark, leathery leaves shaped like fiddles. If you do not have much room, try the dwarf sport 'Phyllis Craig.' Watch out for drafts or sudden temperature changes, which may cause leaf drop.

Mistletoe fig (*F. diversifolia* [*"lutescens"*])—This is a woody shrub form with small, heart-shaped leaves. It is excellent for bonsai training.

Rubber plant *(F. elastica)*—A tree form with large, oblong glossy, dark green leaves, it is an old-fashioned, tough house plant. However, exposure to drafts or sudden temperature change may cause leaf drop.

Rubber plant

The variety *F. elastica* 'Decora' is an excellent cultivar, since it grows slower and is more striking in appearance than most others.

Weeping fig *(F. benjamina)*— This is a beautiful, dense tree whose branches have a drooping habit. Leaves are oval and leathery. 'Exotica' is an excellent cultivar.

Fiddle-leaf fig—see *Ficus*

Firecracker plant *(Crossandra infundibuliformis)*

W, G, 2, M, E. From India comes this small shrub-like evergreen plant with shiny green leaves and spikes of orange-scarlet or salmon-rose flowers. Propagate from cuttings and use bottom heat. They are quite fussy about temperature and humidity. This is a beautiful plant which can provide you with a challenge. A cultivar, 'Mona Wallhed,' is a good choice.

Fishtail palm—see Palm

Fittonia—see Nerve plant

Flame violets (*Episcia species*)

W, G, 2, M, E. Episcias originated in the tropical rain forests of Central and South America. Like African violets, they are members of the gesneriad family, and if you can grow African violets, you can grow episcias in your home. They grow best in 40 to 50 percent humidity, and do very well in greenhouses and

Flame violet

terraria. Flowers will be few if the humidity is low. I have some thriving episcias in my home. If you want foliage only, they will grow under subdued (N) light conditions. They are moderately difficult plants to grow.

Episcias are noted for their exotic foliage which runs through shades of emerald green, silver, iron blue on bronze, to solid bronze. Veins may be contrasting in colors of brown, willow green, silver, cream, or rose, and leaves may be variegated, edged, spotted, or embossed with similar colors. The trumpet-shaped flowers are of many hues such as red, orange-red, orange, pink, yellow, cream, white, light blue, and lavender-blue. Plants are trailers and look fantastic in hanging baskets. Since they can be almost everblooming and have decorative, vining foliage, they are excellent display plants.

Propagation is generally by runners because they produce plants very quickly, although leaves or seeds can be used.

There are many cultivars to choose from. My favorites include some of the cultivars of *Episcia cupreata:* 'Acajou,' 'Chocolate Soldier,' and 'Silver Sheen.' These all have orange or red-orange flowers. A mutant of *E. cupreata,* 'Tropical Topaz,' has yellow flowers. For pink flowers, try 'Pinkiscia.' 'Columbia Orange' has orange flowers, *E. dianthiflora* and 'Cygnet' have white flowers, and *E. lilacina* 'Cuprea' has lavender blue flowers. All of these have beautiful foliage.

For really unusual foliage, try 'Painted Warrior' (silver leaves with pink tinge and dark-green margins), 'Ember Lace' (green and pink), and 'Pink Brocade' (a mixture of silver green, rose pink, and cream). The latter has proved to be fussy in my plant room, but thrives in a fishbowl terrarium.

Flowering maple *(Abutilon)*

I, A, 1, B, E. These tropical South American plants have green or variegated maple-like leaves and hanging bell flowers in hues of white, yellow, apricot, pink, or red. When young, pinch them back to encourage branching; prune them in September to improve flowering. Keeping them potbound also encourages blooming. Propagate them by taking young wood cuttings in the spring or autumn. They are not related to the maple, but to the hollyhock. The cultivars of *A. hybridum* are good choices; they are fairly challenging indoors.

Flowering maple

Fruits—see Chapter 8

Fuchsia—see Ladies' eardrops

Gardenia

W, G, 2, B, E. Most people have heard of this Chinese shrub with its dark glossy leaves and waxy, fragrant, single or double white flowers. It is found outdoors in the deep South. As a pot plant, many people experience trouble with bud drop. The gardenia is a rather sensitive plant, and drafts, alkaline soils, insufficient iron, insufficient humidity, and no night temperature drop can cause bud drop and/or yellowing, falling leaves.

Avoid drafts, and keep the soil acid with a monthly watering of one-half teaspoon vinegar per quart of water. Compost mixed in the potting soil and an extra layer on the surface (see Chapter 3 on fertilizers) should supply enough iron. If you have yellow leaves with green veins, you have an iron deficiency problem called iron chlorosis. Alkaline soil tends to worsen this condition. If your humidity is below 40 percent, you can put a clear plastic bag, such as the ones from dry cleaners, over the plant. Turn your thermostat down at night and keep the plant near a window for night temperature drop, which is essential to prevent bud drop. This sounds like a lot of trouble, but it is worth it to see and smell those blossoms.

Plants from the florist will often be troublesome the first year, but put them outdoors in the summer and they will revive. They should adjust to your conditions when returned to the house. Propagate by softwood summer cuttings or hardwood cuttings of the past year's growth taken in the winter. Try to get *Gardenia jasminoides* 'Veitchii' for your house.

Geranium *(Pelargonium)*

C or I, A, 1, B, D. This genus comprises a colorful group of southern African herbs found in semi-arid regions. Wide diversity is shown in foliage shapes, flower forms and colors (pink, salmon, red, and white), and scents. If they receive too much nitrogen, the foliage becomes lush at the expense of flowers; too much water causes leaf yellowing and rot. Beware of water on leaves—it invites fungal diseases. During the winter, temperatures as low as 50°F are tolerated. Keep geraniums potbound for flowering. Take stem-tip cuttings in the fall for spring and summer flowering; for winter flowering take cuttings in May and debud flowers until the autumn. These plants are not difficult to grow and they have much to offer. There are many species which can be conveniently divided into the following four groups:

Lady Washington group— These are sometimes called show or fancy types, and are cultivars of *P. domesticum.* Their flowers are the largest of all the geraniums, and they are colorful additions to window boxes and patios. During the winter, rest them with cool temperatures (50°F) and less water.

House group—These are also known as fish or zonal geraniums and are cultivars of *P. hortorum.* Leaves are varied and include variegated types. For winter bloom, these cannot be beat. There are hundreds of excellent cultivars.

Ivy-leaved group—Of vine-like habit, these cultivars of *P. peltatum* can be pinched back so that they can be kept under control. If they bloom, they do so from late winter to early fall.

Ivy-leaved geranium

Scented-leaved group —These have fragrant leaves whose odor is released by gently rubbing the foliage. Leaf shape is diverse. Some of the scents are lemon *(P. crispum)*, rose *(P. graveolens)*, apple *(P. odoratissimum)*, peppermint *(P. tomentosum)*, apricot *(P. scabrum)*, ginger *(P. torento)*, lime *(P. nervosum)*, and pine *(P. denticulatum)*.

Gesneria—see Gesneriads

Gesneriads

Generally W, G, 2, M, E. There are roughly 125 genera and at least 2000 species in the gesneriad family, not to mention innumerable hybrids. With all these candidates, it is not surprising that some have tubers, others rhizomes, and some fibrous roots. While most derive from the tropics, there are even some semi-hardy gesneriads. There is something in the gesneriad family for the beginner, the successful hobbyist, and the advanced grower looking for a challenge.

The following fibrous-rooted gesneriads are discussed elsewhere under individual headings: African violets *(Saintpaulia)*, lipstick plant *(Aeschynanthus)*, Goldfish plant *(Columnea)*, flame violet *(Episcia)*, *Hypocyrta, Nautilocalyx,* and Cape Primrose *(Streptocarpus)*.

Separate headings for rhizome types include Magic flower *(Achimenes)*, *Kohleria,* and Temple Bells *(Smithiantha)*. Those with tubers under separate headings are gloxinia *(Sinningia speciosa)* and *Rechsteineria*.

The above, listed under separate headings, are the more common house plant gesneriads. Naturally, there are many more, such as the following, which might supply some very unusual choices for advanced house plant lovers. Unless otherwise specified, they are coded as W, G, 2, M, E.

Alloplectus—A. capitatus—(large green leaves, yellow flowers, bright red calyx) and *A. vittatus* (similar flowers, maroon foliage) are good upright species. *A. ambiguus* and *A. domingensis* (smaller leaves, yellow flowers) are suitable for hanging baskets. These tropical American plants are somewhat fussy bloomers. Propagate by stem or leaf cuttings, or start from seeds.

*Bellonia—*This   easy-to-grow trailer with small leaves comes from the West Indies. It has white flowers and is easily propagated from tip cuttings. *B. spinosa* has the distinction of being the only gesneriad with thorns.

Boea—This east Asian gesneriad varies, but the best for indoor cultivation is *B. hygroscopica,* which has a rosette of light green, hairy leaves. Flowers are blue and resemble African violets. Propagate from seed or leaf cuttings. They grow very well under fluorescent lamps.

Briggsia—C, A, 2, M, D. This is semi-hardy and suited to a cool porch, a summer patio, or an alpine house. The best known is *B. muscicola.*

Chirita—This native of India is about as easy to grow as an African violet. *C. senensis* is best; it has a rosette of leaves laced with silver and light orchid-colored blooms. Propagate from leaf or tip cuttings. *C. micromusa* is also easy to grow with yellow-orange flowers and seed capsules resembling hands of bananas.

Chrysothemis—These have tubers, thin green leaves, attractive yellow-red striped flowers, and attractive calyces which may remain for two or three months. Try *C. pulchella* or *C. friedrichsthaliana.* Propagate from tip cuttings and watch for the dormancy period.

Codonanthe—This resembles the lipstick plant, but has red dots on leaf undersides; it grows as easily as *Columnea* and is excellent for hanging baskets. Propagate from tip cuttings. You might try *C. crassifolia* or *C. macradenia.*

Conandron—C, A, 2, M, D. This Japanese gesneriad has a rosette of leaves and violet flowers. It is excellent for semi-heated sun porches. Propagate from seed or offset division.

Diastema—These small plants with rhizomes are similar to the smaller *Achimenes.* Try *D. quinquevulnerum.*

Gesneria—These gesneriads from the West Indies can become large. Smaller ones, such as *G. cuneifolia,* which are characterized by their shiny green leaves and red firecracker blossoms, do well in a terrarium. Propagate from seed or by division.

Gloxinia—Do not confuse this plant with the plant whose common name is gloxinia and whose scientific name is *Sinningia speciosa.* The best is *G. perennis* from Columbia. It has rhizomes, reddish green leaves, and bell-like lavender blooms.

Koellikeria—You might try the tropical American *K. erinoides* with rosette-forming leaves and whitish red flowers. This compact plant appears delicate. It has rhizomes. Try it in a terrarium.

Petrocosmea—These southeast Asian gesneriads form a rosette of leaves and have white, purple, or yellow flowers similar to African violets. Propagate from leaf cuttings or division. They are a challenge to bring into bloom. Try *P. kerrii* or *P. parryorum*.

Phinaea—This miniature gesneriad *(P. multiflora)* is a tropical American beauty which is at home in a terrarium. Grow from seed and remove dead blossoms. Flowers are small and white.

Seemannia—These South American gesneriads do well under fluorescent lights. They have rhizomes, bright green leaves, and red or yellow bell-shaped flowers. Propagate from cuttings. Try *S. latifolia* and *S. sylvatica*.

These suggestions should keep you busy. There are many others far too numerous to mention. Then of course there is always hybridization, which, with the gesneriad family, could provide a lifetime hobby for the amateur. For those interested in more gesneriads and hybridization, consult the Bibliography.

Ginger—see Common ginger

Glorybower *(Clerodendrum thomsonae)*

W, G, 1, M, E. These are vigorous vines from tropical Africa which have lush green, large, papery leaves. Flowers are crimson with creamy white outer petals. During the winter decrease watering and lower temperature if possible. Try them in a hanging basket. Propagate from cuttings of half-ripe wood and prune them vigorously to prevent a scraggly appearance and to induce flowering.

Gloxinia—see Gesneriads (do not confuse with common gloxinia below)

Gloxinia *(Sinningia speciosa)*

W, G, 2, M, E. Gloxinias (not to be confused with the *Gloxinia perennis,* another gesneriad) are the second most popular member of the gesneriad family. These tropical South American plants are not too difficult to grow. Planted as tubers, they are easily propagated from seeds or leaf cuttings. When watering, avoid cold water on leaves, which causes spots. Flowers are spectacular in upright inverted bells or nodding slipper types in red, blue, purple, or white. Some are speckled, and they can be single or double. When flowers are finished blooming, decrease water until leaves dry and store the pots in a dark, cool cellar (60°F). After six to 10 weeks (during which time you should water only two or three

times), repot and increase watering
and exposure to light.

There is a wide range of cultivars to choose from. For large flowers, the florist gloxinia hybrids are
breath-taking and require a lot of
room. Dwarf varieties of the florist
gloxinia are available. For miniature
gloxinias to grow in a brandy snifter
or terrarium, try *S. pusilla, S. pusilla*
'White Sprite,' and *S. concinna.*
These reach a size of about two-by-
two inches. Some excellent miniatures slightly larger than these are
'Bright Eyes,' 'Doll baby,' and
'Freckles.' If older stems are
removed after flowering, these
miniatures may blossom for over a
year.

Goldfish plant *(Columnea)*

W, G, 2, M, E. These colorful
members of the gesneriad family require about the same environment
and are as easy to grow as the African violet. Foliage is usually velvety
green, sometimes with purple hairs.
The tubular flowers that have an
overhanging upper lobe, are red,
yellow, pink, or orange; they resemble flying goldfish. Flowers appear
in the spring, summer, and fall.
Some cultivars are upright and others are trailers. The latter make
lovely hanging basket plants. These
tropical Central and South American natives are easily propagated
from stem cuttings.

Some interesting cultivars include 'Joy,' 'Yellow Dragon,' 'Gol-
die,' 'Campus Queen,' and 'Katsura'

(variegated foliage). Of course there are many more cultivars. A few, like *C. microphylla,* 'Stavanger,' and *C. hirta,* need lower temperatures or short day lengths to start flowers.

Grape ivy, kangaroo vine *(Cissus)*

I, A, 1, M, D. *Cissus* comes from the various tropical regions of the world. Related to the grape, it is a vining plant which climbs with the aid of tendrils. As such, it is good for trellis training and hanging baskets. It's fairly tolerant and makes a good house plant. Pinch the growing tips to keep it shaped. Propagation is by cuttings.

Grape Ivy

The best varieties for the house are *C. rhombifolia* (grape ivy) and *C. antarctica* (kangaroo vine). Grape ivy has toothed compound leaves (three leaflets) and kangaroo vine has large toothed leaves. A miniature version of kangaroo vine, *C. anarctica* 'Minima', is better for the house than the standard type.

Greigia sphacelata

I, A, 4, B, D. This Chilean bromeliad is plain with its leathery, glossy green leaves and little rose-colored flowers. It is one of the few ground dwelling bromeliads. (See bromeliads for more information.)

Grevillea robusta—see Silk oak

Gymnocalycium—see Cacti

Gynura aurantiaca—see Velvet plant

Hare's foot fern, Hart's tongue fern—see
Ferns

Haworthia

I, A, 3, M, D. These are succulents (see Succulents also) from
southern Africa. The thick, fleshy
leaves form basal rosettes flecked
with white dots or cross bands. Leaf
color varies from blue-green to
gray-green to black-green and even
purple-brown. They are rather attractive plants, and are tough and
adaptable to various situations.
Propagate them by offsets or cuttings. There are many species; the
following ones may interest you:

Haworthia

> *H. fasciata*—Small rosettes of
> dark green and pointed leaves
> with cross bands of white dots
> characterize this species. This
> one is commonly available.

> *H. margaritifers*—Blackishgreen
> rosettes covered with creamy
> tubercles make this one stand
> out in the crowd.

Hedera—see Ivy

Helxine soleirollii—see Baby's tears

Herbs—see Chapter 8

Hippeastrum—see Amaryllis

Holiday cacti

W, A, 4, M, E, (April through
September) and I or C, A, 4, M, D,
(October through March). There
are three basic holiday cacti: Christ-
mas, Thanksgiving, and Easter.
Each will be discussed below. All

are epiphytes or tree crotch dwellers from the South American tropical forests. During the spring and summer they require more water than most cacti, but during the fall and winter, watering two to four times a month is sufficient. For better blooms, they should be kept somewhat pot-bound. Holiday cacti are not difficult to grow, and their floral beauty is overwhelming at a time when other house plant flowers are at a low ebb. Propagation is by rooting cuttings each of which should contain at least two jointed segments.

Holiday cactus in bloom

Difficulty in getting holiday cacti to bloom is a frequent complaint. Since they are short-day plants, it is not surprising. One sure way is to subject them to darkness from 6:00 P.M. to 8:00 A.M., beginning on September 1 and lasting until bud formation. And they must be put in total darkness—either by keeping them in a room that is kept dark at night or by putting them into a closet every night.

Keeping them always dark at night was difficult for me, so I found an alternative, one that works quite well. At temperatures of 50° to 55° F or slightly lower, these cacti lose their short-day requirement for flower bud setting, and become day-length neutral plants (see Chapter 6). Therefore I leave my plants outside until frost threatens (but not when frost comes—frost will kill them) so that they are subjected to nighttime temperatures of 45° to

55°F for four weeks. This assures flower bud production. I bring them in the house and do not worry about lights or closets. All my holiday cacti bloomed when I used this method. If the weather won't allow you to leave the cacti outdoors, try putting them in a cool east cellar window, breezeway, cool attic or similar location.

Christmas cactus *(Schlumbergera bridgesii)—S. bridgesii* is the old-fashioned Christmas cactus your grandmother grew. It is characterized by glossy, green, flat segments joined in a chain-like manner. These form a pendant mound of foliage. The characteristic that is indicative of the *Schlumbergera* genus is the rounded tips on the leaf segments. Flowers are pendant and usually red or reddish orange.

Easter cactus *(Rhipsalidopsis gaertneri)*—For nearly 60 years, this had been incorrectly known as *Schlumbergera gaertneri.* It has thicker, narrower leaf segments, and less pronounced leaf margin detail than Christmas or Thanksgiving cacti. Flowers, which appear around Easter, are scarlet and star-shaped. It is a bit more troublesome than the Christmas or Thanksgiving cactus, since it needs cool temperatures (40° to 60°F) during the winter in order to bloom.

Thanksgiving cactus *(Zygocactus truncatus)*—This is sometimes called crab cactus. It differs from *Schlumbergera* in that it blossoms slightly earlier and has pointed, not rounded, tips or teeth on the leaf segments, especially on the blunt apex. Flowers are usually scarlet with white undertones.

Of course hybrids and cultivars of the above species have been produced, which add to nomenclature problems. One famous authority now feels that *Zygocactus truncatus* should really be *Schlumbergera truncatus*. However, it makes no difference what their name is; they are beautiful and should be grown on that merit alone.

Howeia—see Palms

Hoya carnosa—see Wax plant

Hylocereus—see Cacti

Hypocyrta

W, G, 2, M, E. *Hypocyrta,* a trailing plant suited to hanging baskets, is a member of the gesneriad family which originated in tropical Central and South America. They are about as easy to grow as African violets. They have bright green leaves and small, pouch-shaped flowers in shades of orange and red. Take tip cuttings after flowers are finished for easy propagation and to promote branching. You might try

H. nummularia, H. strigulosa, or the new hybrid, 'Tropicana.'

Hypoestes sanguinolenta—see Polka dot plant

Impatiens—see Patience plant

Ivy *(Hedera)*

C, or I, A, 1, B, E. Ivy is an evergreen woody vine that originated in Europe, north Africa, and Asia. Undoubtedly, early American settlers brought it here. Ivy is a tenacious climber that is aided by its aerial rootlets. So long as its cultural requirements are met, it does reasonably well in a home—in a hanging basket, on a trellis or topiary form, or just hanging over a pot rim. Pinch ivy to encourage branching and propagate it from cuttings.

There are only a few species, such as *H. canariensis* (Algerian ivy), *H. colchica aurea* (Golden Persian ivy), and *H. helix* (English ivy). The latter has been naturalized in the United States and is the species most commonly found in homes. At least 50 cultivars of English ivy are available. There are many variegated types and many variations in leaf size, shape, and form.

H. helix 'Scutifolia' *("cordata")* has heart-shaped, dark green leaves (heart-leaf ivy); *H. helix* 'Pedata' (bird's foot ivy) has dainty bird's foot-shaped leaves; *H. helix hibernica* (Irish ivy) is larger and more vigorous than English ivy; *H. helix* 'Hahn's self-branching' tends to branch quite freely, forming a dense

mat; *H. helix* 'Hahn's variegated' is
an excellent variegated form with
silver-gray edged with white; *H.
helix* 'Fluffy Ruffles' has crested, un-
dulated leaves; *H. helix* 'Needlepoint' has tiny, elongated, three-
lobed leaves and is a dwarf; *H. helix*
'Walthamensis' (Baby ivy) has tiny,
deep green leaves; and *H. helix*
'Marginata' has gray-green leaves
margined in white.

Ivy-leaved geranium—see Geranium

Jade plant—see *Crassula*

Jerusalem cherry *(Solanum pseudocapsicum)*

I, A, 1, B, D. This is a shrubby
plant from Madeira. Pointed oval
leaves form a dense green cover
which is set off by small, white, star-
like flowers. Many florists sell this
plant around Christmas. The
orange-scarlet cherries appear in the
fall; they are globular in shape and
about one-half inch in diameter.
Since they are poisonous, Jerusalem
cherries and children should not
mix. This plant is somewhat fussy
and may not do well in your home,
especially if it comes from a florist.
During the summer, you can cut it
back and place it outdoors, but be
sure to bring it in before frost. Start
it from seed in early March if you
want to get late fall fruit. The dwarf
variety 'Pattersonii' is best.

Kafir lily *(Clivia miniata)*

I, A, 1, M, D. These bulb-like
plants with fleshy roots come from

South Africa. Leaves are long, arching, waxy, and strap-like. Bell-shaped flowers appear in early spring. They are orange-scarlet in color and are borne in clusters on erect flower stalks. If you want flowers, keep the plants pot-bound. Water them sparingly in the winter. Their culture is very similar to that of the amaryllis. Since they dislike being disturbed, you can leave them in the same pot for five years. Scratch out and replace the top third of the soil each year. When you finally repot them, you can propagate them by division.

Kafir lily

Kalanchoe

I, A, 3, B, D. These succulent plants of Africa and India usually have waxy green leaves, which, in some species, are toothed. It is a good house plant because it seems to adapt itself to most environments. Propagate from cuttings (air-dry 24 hours prior to rooting) or seeds. Refer to Succulents for more details. Sometimes certain *Kalanchoe* are known as *"Bryophyllum"*, although *Kalanchoe* is the preferred scientific name. Some interesting species you might try follow:

Kalanchoe

   K. blossfeldiana var. 'Tom Thumb'—This is the familiar plant, covered with red flower heads, which is found at the florist at Christmastime. This is a short-day plant, and its flowers may appear later than December 25, unless they receive darkness from 6:00 P.M. until 7:00 A.M. starting in September. Leaves are waxy and toothed; the flowers last a month or more.

K. daigremontiana ("Bryophyllum")—This is very easy to grow. It has arching, long, tricornered leaves which produce many small plantlets at the serrated leaf margins. The plantlets will root by themselves if they come in contact with the soil.

K. pinnata ("Bryophyllum")—This is sometimes known as the air plant or living leaf, because the young plantlets can develop from the scalloped leaves, even when detached from the parent plant.

K. tomentosa (Panda plant)—These have leaves covered with dense, white felt and some brown spots.

Kangaroo vine—see Grape ivy

Koellikeria—see Gesneriads

Kohleria

W, G, 2, M, E. These upright and sometimes trailing tropical American plants are members of the gesneriad family. They are about as easy to grow as African violets. The

Panda plant

attractive foliage is sometimes hairy. Tubular flowers are red, orange, yellow, pink, or purple and are often spotted. Unless you continuously remove old growth, they often lapse into dormancy during the winter. Propagation is by root cuttings or rhizome division. Desirable hybrids are 'Cecelia, 'Lonwood,' 'Rongo;' the species *K. amabilis, K. bogotensis, K. eriantha,* and *K. lindeniana* are also attractive.

Ladies' eardrops *(Fuchsia* x *hybrida)*

I, A, 1, M, E. These are the cultivated fuchsias which derive from several species coming from the Central and South American tropics. Twigs are sturdy and covered with dark green, pointed, oval leaves. Flowers are large, gay, and pendant with showy stamens. Flowering is best from March through November; the colors of the flowers are pink, red, rose, blue, fuchsia, and white. They are naturals for hanging baskets; pinch them early to develop bushy plants. Propagation is by cuttings. Rest the plants during the winter by keeping the soil somewhat drier than usual. And, if possible, keep them at lower temperatures—at about 50°F. Although these are somewhat troublesome, their beauty more than makes up for the extra effort they might need.

Lady palm—see Palm

Laelia—see Orchids

Lemon—see *Citrus*

Lime—see *Citrus*

Lipstick plant *(Aeschynanthus)*

W, G, 2, M, E. These trailing plants, which are native to southeast Asia, are members of the gesneriad family. However, they are a little more tricky to get to blossom than the African violet, but are well worth the effort. They are excellent for hanging baskets. Leaves are waxy green. The orange or red tubular flowers that emerge from the calyces resemble a tube of lipstick.

Lipstick plant

After flowering, which can be almost all year 'round under optimal conditions, cut them back to the stems to promote branching. Save those cut-off stems for propagation. The flowers are rather temperamental and fall off if the air is too dry or hot. You might try 'Black Pagoda,' *A. pulcher*, or *A. lobbianus*

Lithops—see Living stones

Living leaf—see *Kalanchoe*

Living stones *(Lithops)*

I, A, 3, B, D. These are very small, peculiar South African succulents which resemble small stones. Leaves are usually joined pairs, giving the impression of a grooved pebble on the soil surface. The surface part of the plant is covered with window-like structures which allow sun-

Living stone

light to reach the chlorophyll-containing cells. Colors are varied, but gray and white are the most common. The yellow or white flowers are quite attractive and appear from the groove on the plant surface. Go very easy on fertilizer and water with these plants: during the winter they require no water or practically none. Propagation is by seed. Although these are more difficult to grow than most succulents, their uniqueness makes them worth growing.

Living-vase plant, Air pine *(Aechmea)*

W, A, 4, M, E. These Central and South American plants are members of the bromeliad family. *Aechmea* are easy to raise with moderate care and make a good choice for your first bromeliads. The arching, strap-like leaves form a cup in which water must always be kept. Change this water every two weeks and keep the soil evenly moist. Leaves are variegated, deep red, or very shiny. Flower spikes have brilliantly colored bracts and insignificant flowers. Berries of bright hues, which last for a few months, also appear. When you fertilize, use weak fish emulsion sparingly and add it to the "water cup." The mother plant produces offsets which can be cut and rooted after they are two inches or longer. You might try the following species:

Living vase plant

A. chantinii—Leaves have pink-ish-gray bands and red bracts with yellow tips.

A. fasciata—Flower heads are rose and blue and tufted.

A. marmorata (Grecian vase plant)—Leaves are mottled and have pink bracts with blue flowers.

'Foster's Favorite'—Hybrid with wine red leaves and red and blue flowers. It makes an excellent house plant.

Magic flower *(Achimenes)*

W, G, 2, M, E. These plants are members of the gesneriad family, and their culture is somewhat related to that of African violets. They are not well known by many gardeners. *Achimenes* have glossy, hairy, cut-leaf foliage and petunia-like flowers in shades of white, yellow pink, blue, and violet. Some are upright and others are trailers. They are native to the Central American tropics.

They are propagated from rhizomes (around January), stem cuttings, or seeds. When they are about two inches high, pinch them back to encourage branching. *Achimenes,* which are started from rhizomes in January, will bloom in the summer and fall; they make excellent hanging basket or pot plants for the sun room, window, porch, and patio. When fall arrives, they can continue their blossoming indoors. *Achimenes* enter a dormant period in the late fall, and their rhizomes are held dormant until January. During this time keep them cool, on the dry side, and in dim light.

Some hybrids which you might try include 'Crimson Glory,' 'Wetterlows Triumph,' 'Yellow Beauty,' and 'Ambroise Verschaffelt' to name just a few. If you can grow African violets, most likely you will succeed with *Achimenes.*

Maidenhair fern—see Ferns

Malpighia coccigera—see Miniature holly

Mammillaria—see Cacti

Maranta leuconeura kerchoveana—see Prayer plant

Measle plant—see Polka-dot plant

Meat-eating plants

Most of the meat-eating plants live in boggy areas, where they trap and digest insects with the aid of digestive fluids. Their sustenance comes from the protein they extract from the insects. Some of these plants rely on bacteria instead of digestive fluids to decompose the insects, and in such cases, steal the protein from the bacteria. At home you can substitute a bit of ground beef or egg white in place of insects. Many of these plants can be found in the east and west coast bogs of our country. Generally they only do well in a terrarium; they look very nice in one when mixed with some ferns and mosses to create a minia-

ture bog. You can add some sphagnum moss to the humus lover's soil
mix to get a bog-like soil. Some of
the more common carnivorous
plants follow:

Butterwort *(Pinguicula)*—I, G,
2, N, S. This genus can be
found in bogs in Mexico and
North America. *P. vulgaris* is
native to our country and *P.
caudata* and *P. gypsicola* are
found in Mexico. They all rely
on a sticky digestive fluid to
trap insects. *P. vulgaris* and *P.
caudata* have rosettes of sticky
oval leaves, and *P. gypsicola* has
rosettes of narrow, linear,
sticky, hairy leaves. Flowers are
purple and red respectively.

Cobra plant*(Darlingtonia cali-
fornica)*—C, G, 2, N, S. These
bog plants are found in California and Oregon. The leaves
form light green, hooded pitchers which resemble a cobra and
have downward-pointing hairs
to trap the insects. Flowers are
purple. They rely on bacteria
for digestion.

Pitcher plant *(Sarracenia)*—C,
G, 2, B, S. This genus is found
in North American bogs. Most
have leaf pitchers with trapping
hairs and a honey-like bait.
There are several species.

Sundew *(Drosera)*—C, G, 2, B,
S. These have hairy leaves with
glistening drops of a sticky substance to trap the insect. Once

the insect is trapped, the hair-like tentacles close around him. *D. filiformis* and *D. rotundifolia* both have small white flowers and are found in North American bogs.

Venus flytrap *(Dionaea muscipula)*—C, G, 2, B, S. Of all the carnivorous bog plants, these are the best known. These are found in Carolina bogs, where their leafy rosettes have a beartrap-like arrangement at the ends. These toothed traps snap shut on any insect unlucky enough to land in them.

Venus flytrap

Medicine plant, Burn plant *(Aloe vera);* Partridge Breast plant *(Aloe variegata)*

I, A, 3, B, D. *Aloe vera* (vera means true, hence true aloe) is a gray-green, stemless, cactus-like plant common to Cape Verde, the Canary Islands, and Madeira. It is not, however, a cactus; it is a succulent belonging to the lily family. The waxy leaves are lance-shaped (flat on top and slightly rounded underneath) and grow in a rosette formation. Sparse blunt spines and white spots appear on the leaves, which can grow up to two feet long. Blossoms are insignificant yellow cylinders. They appear infrequently, but if you wish, you might successfully force some blossoms by enclosing the plant and a ripe apple in a plastic bag for several days.

Stripping the thin, green skin

Burn plant *(Aloe vera)*

reveals a clear gel which is used in the treatment of burns and skin ailments, thus the origin of its common name. The juice and gel are also used in some cosmetics.

As a house plant, it rates high because it is attractive, easy to raise, and slow growing. *Aloe vera* is adaptable and will tolerate the less-than-optimal conditions found in apartments. Let the soil dry thoroughly between waterings. Propagation is achieved by rooting suckers, which have been air-dried for 24 hours.

Partridge breast

The *Aloe* genus has an extensive number of species. One of these (also popular as a house plant) is *Aloe variegata,* commonly called partridge breast plant. It is common to the Cape of Good Hope. The triangular, blue-green leaves, which grow up to 12 inches long, have cross-banded white spots. Blooms are tubular and salmon red. Its treatment and adaptibility is similar to that of *Aloe vera.*

Mexican breadfruit *(Monstera deliciosa)*

W, A, 1, M, E. This tropical Central American plant is also known as Swiss cheese plant or ceriman. Long, cord-like aerial roots hang from the stems. In its mature form it has large leathery leaves which are cut and perforated with oblong holes, but in its juvenile stage, the leaves are smaller and less perforated. The latter form is often sold as *Philodendron pertusum.* Mature plants produce a cone-like edible fruit, which has a pineapple

Mexican breadfruit

aroma. However, as a house plant, the development of fruit is unlikely. The fruit must be ripe when eaten because the unripe form contains a chemical which will cause the mouth to swell painfully. These plants are attractive, especially when trained on a bark slab, and are not difficult to grow. Propagate from stem cuttings.

Meyer lemon—see *Citrus*

Milk bush—see *Euphorbia*

Mimosa pudica—see Sensitive plant

Miniature holly *(Malpighia coccigera)*

    I, A, 1, B, D. As a house plant, this is fairly tolerant. It is a bushy evergreen shrub from the West Indies, which has a dense covering of holly-like leaves that are glossy, dark green, and have coarse, spiny teeth. Flowers are small and pink; fruits are red. Propagate from cuttings. It makes a nice bonsai when properly trained.

Mistletoe fig—see *Ficus*

Monstera deliciosa—see Mexican breadfruit

'Moon Valley Plant' (*Pilea* 'Moon Valley')

    W, A, 1, M, E. This vegetative sport originated from an unknown species of *Pilea*. It was developed in a greenhouse by a shrewd businessman who realized the new plant's potential and quickly patented it. I have observed that it is now a standard supermarket plant. Like other *Pilea* (see aluminum plant) it is easily propagated by cuttings.

Moon valley plant

Leaves are hairy and arched; the edges and pointed peaks are light green in color, and the valleys are a rich chocolate-bronze. Stems become bronzy as they mature. It is almost continuously covered with stalks headed by several clumps of tiny, blushing pink flowers. During the winter it tends to remain small and compact (under one foot) with a minimum of pinching.

Moses-in-the-cradle   (*Rhoeo   spathacea* [*"discolor"*])

Moses in the cradle

I, A, 1, M, E. Native to Mexico, this plant has a rosette of stiff, waxy, lance-shaped leaves which are dark green on top and purple underneath. Little white flowers appear in boat-shaped bracts at the leaf bases. It is quite easy to grow as a house plant. Propagate it from cuttings or seeds. The variety, *vittatus*, has purple leaves with yellow striping.

Mother-in-law tongue—see Snake plant

Mother-of-thousands—see   Piggyback plant

Myrtleleaf orange—see Citrus

Natal plum *(Carissa grandiflora)*

I, A, 1, B, E. In southern California and Florida these plants are often seen as hedges. They make excellent house plants, and are ideal for bonsai. They are evergreen shrubs with fragrant, white, star-shaped flowers and dark, shiny leaves. The flowers are followed by red berries. Of medium difficulty to grow, the natal plum requires pruning to keep a good shape. It is easily propagated from cuttings.

Nautilocalyx

W, G, 2, M, E. These erect plants, noted for their showy foliage, are members of the gesneriad family. Native to the South American tropics, they have large olive green, pebbly leaves, shiny reddish green leaves, or waxy green leaves with red veins. Flowers are tubular in pale yellow or white colors. They are as easy to grow as African violets. Pinch tips to encourage bushiness, and propagate them by tip cuttings. Species of interest are *N. bullatus, N. forgetti,* and *N. lynchii.*

Necklace vine—see *Crassula*

Neoregelia

W, A, 4, M, E. These bromeliads make good house plants; they are noted for the lovely colors of their leaves which develop prior to flowering and which become pronounced during flowering. Flowers appear near the bottom of the "water cup" and are poor seconds to the colorful foliage. *N. spectabilis* is a good choice. Refer to bromeliads for more information.

Nephrolepsis—see Ferns

Nephthytis *(Syngonium)*

W, A, 1, M, E. *Syngonium* are often confused with the plant whose scientific name is *Nephthytis,* because of the great similarity in their appearance. However, most plants sold in this country as Nephthytis are really *Syngonium.* They are tough durable plants, and are able to tolerate conditions different from those recommended above. In the juvenile stage, they are upright with green or variegated lance- or arrow-shaped leaves; when mature, they become trailers or climbers and develop lobes on their leaves. Since I prefer the immature, upright form, I take stem cuttings of the vine when it appears and start a new plant. They are native to the Central American tropics. Many species are available, the most common being *S. podophyllum* and its cultivars.

Nephthytis

Nerium oleander—see Oleander

Nerve plant *(Fittonia)*

W, G, 2, M, E. This Peruvian plant has thin, oval, vivid green leaves finely netted with white or red veins. Since it is rather fussy about humidity, I keep it in a terrarium. However, it thrives so well there that I must constantly prune it to make it fit its container. I save these cuttings, though, because they

Nerve plant

root easily. *F. vershaffeltii* has red veins and the varieties *F. vershaffeltii argyroneura* and *pearcei* have white and rose-pink veins respectively. The white-veined one is my favorite.

Norfolk Island pine *(Araucaria excelsa)*

Norfolk Island Pine

I, A, 2, M, E. Not a true pine, this evergreen comes from a small island near New Zealand. It has a resemblance to a traditional Christmas tree, but it is much more graceful in appearance. Norfolk Island pine makes an interesting and fairly tolerant house plant. Do not prune it—if you remove the terminal leader, it loses much of its graceful shape. Propagation is from seed or a terminal leader cutting. Rooted side cuttings grow into misshapen plants.

Notocactus—see Cacti

Oleander *(Nerium oleander)*

I, A, 1, B, E. These evergreen Mediterranean shrubs have willowy branches with whorls of long, narrow leathery leaves. Different varieties have red, pink, or white single and double flowers. These are more patio or summer porch plants, since they are summer bloomers. When flowering is completed, prune the plant back to wood (take about one-third off) to induce new vegetative growth. Then put it into a cool, frost-free place to winter over, and give it an occasional watering. Bring it outdoors in May.

'Album' has white flowers, 'Atropurpureum' has single red blooms, and 'Variegatum' has gray-green leaves edged in creamy white and red-rose flowers. It is easy to grow. If you do not object to winter storage, it is a nice summer tub plant.

Oncidium—see Orchids

Opuntia—see Cacti

Orange—see Citrus

Orchids

Who does not know these tropical beauties with their stunning blossoms? There are literally thousands of species and hybrids; it is no wonder that many beginning orchid growers soon lose interest in other house plants and become orchid specialists.

Orchids generally like high humidity, moderate levels of sunlight, and a moisture-retaining growing medium such as osmunda fiber or shredded fir bark. Some will grow in soil rich in humus. Temperature requirements are quite varied for the many cultivars. Many orchids have a short dormancy period. Most thrive under fluorescent lights.

Those orchids which form pseudo-bulbs (food storage stems) may be propagated from surface rhizome cuttings. Orchids without pseudo-bulbs are propagated from stem cuttings, some can be propagated by division.

Although there are many orchids, I recommend the following for beginners:

Cattleya—I, G, (Osmunda) M, D. These are the common corsage orchids. They are usually big purple-white flowers, but other colors, such as yellow, are also found in this genus. It is probably the easiest orchid for the beginner.

Cypripedium—C, G, 4, M, E. Known as the lady's slipper orchid, these are small and attractive, as well as adaptable.

Epidendrum—I, and S, G, (osmunda) M, D. These come in all sizes and shapes; they are very tolerant plants.

Laelia—C, and I, G, (osmunda) M, D. These have star-shaped flowers in many colors. They are quite tolerant.

Oncidium—I, and S, G, (osmunda) M, D. Known as the dancing lady orchids, these are varied and beautiful.

Phalaenopsis—W, G, (osmunda) N, E. Often used in bridal bouquets, these are not quite as easy to grow as the others.

For a bit more challenge, you might try *Miltonia, Catasetum, Lockhartia,* or *Maxillaria* in your house.

Osmanthus fragrans—see Sweet olive

Otaheite orange—see Citrus

Oxalis—see Wood sorrel

Palms

Graceful feathery foliage and fan-shaped leaves are characteristic of these tropical trees. Those with feathery foliage are smaller and tend to make better house plants in places where space is limited. Since palms do not branch, damage to the terminal leader results in the eventual death of the stem. Propagation is usually by seed; however, the young plants are usually unattractive so most people prefer to purchase established plants. A few types of palms can be propagated by division. There are many genera in the Palmaceae family, but those which make good, tolerant house plants are described below:

Caryota—W, A, 1, M, S. These are clumping palms with scalloped foliage on tall stems. *C. mitis* is known as the clustered fishtail palm and *C. urens* as the fishtail palm.

Chamaedorea—W, A, 1, N, E. Most of these form clumps and have feathery foliage. The popular parlor palm comes from this group; *C. elegans ("Collinia")*, it also comes in a miniature variety called 'bella' *("Neanthe bella")*.

Chrysalidocarpus—W, A, 1, M, S. These are graceful, feathery clump-forming palms. The best

Palm "Neanthe bella"

is the butterfly palm or *C. lutescens* *("Areca")*.

Howeia *("Kentia")*—I, A, 1, M, E. These feathery palms are attractive. The sentry palm *(H. belmoreana)* and paradise palm *(H. forsteriana)* are prominent species.

Rhapis—I, A, 1, M, S. These have a reedy, oriental look. From this genus, the lady palm *(R. excelsa)* makes a good choice.

Pan-American friendship plant—see Aluminum plant

Pandanus—see Screw pine

Panda plant—see *Kalanchoe*

Paradise palm—see Palms

Parlor palm—see Palms

Partridge breast plant—see Medicine plant

Passiflora—see Passion vine

Passion vine *(Passiflora)*

Passion vine

W, G, 1, B, E. These vigorous vining plants are found in the warmer parts of the United States, Central America, and South America. Rather large and fussy, most do poorly in houses. However, I have found one type, *Passiflora* x *alatocaerulea,* a hybrid between *P. alato* and *P. caerulea,* that blooms indoors. During January one flower on my plant opened for 24 hours. The leaves are tri-lobed and the fragrant four-inch blossom had white sepals,

pink petals, and a fringed crown of
purple, white, and blue. Propagate
them from seeds or cuttings.

Patience plant *(Impatiens)*

I, A, 2, B, E. Natives
of Africa and New Guinea,
these plants have succulent
stems and colorful flowers
in pink, white, red, or
orange. The species for
house plants is *I. holstii.* It
blooms rather freely, and
many colorful hybrids are
available. Keep them
pinched to develop a bushy
plant. Indoors these may
get fussy and show their
displeasure by a "leggy" appearance and decreased blooming. They
are easily propagated from seeds or
cuttings. Hanging baskets are the
best way to show them off.

Patience plant

Peacock plant *(Calathea makoyana)*

W, G, 2, M, E. These highly
decorative foliage plants come from
tropical South America. Lines and
ovals of olive green on a pale, yellow-green field give the leaves an
attractive appearance. Propagate by
crown or tuber division. These and
other equally beautiful species of
Calathea do poorly in homes because of insufficient humidity; I
recommend you try one in a terrarium.

Pedilanthus   tithymaloides—see   Devil's
backbone

Pelargonium—see Geraniums

Pellaea—see Ferns

Pellionia

W, G, 1, M, E. From southeast Asia come these attractive ground-hugging creepers. They are characterized by pinkish stems, small oval leaves, and a slow rate of growth. Closely related to *Pilea,* they can be propagated by stem cuttings. In hanging baskets this plant is at its best. Three species are available, but they are difficult to find. The best is *P. daveauana;* it has grayish-green leaves edged with brown-purple to black.

Pellionia

Peperomia

W, A, 1, M, D. There are many varied species in this group of Central and South American tropical plants. Some have small leaves, others big leaves, some are vines, but most are upright, and many are low growers. Most bear flowers which appear as unusual whitish green to green catkins. Quite tolerant to abuse, except to overwatering, these plants will succeed in difficult places. They are easily propagated from stem or leaf cuttings. Some good species for house plants follow:

Peperomia (clockwise from front left): P. obtusifolia variegata, P. obtusifolia, P. nivalis, P. griseoargentia

P. caperata 'Emerald Ripple'— This cultivar has dense clusters of roundish, heart-shaped leaves which are corrugated. The hills are waxy green and the valleys are chocolate brown. A smaller cultivar, "Little Fantasy," is even better.

P. griseo-argentea ("hederaefolia")—Leaves are rounded, quilted with glassy silver on green, and produced in a busy rosette. Veins have a purplish olive cast.

P. nivalis—An attractive, low-clustering plant with many branches that bear small, keel-shaped, slightly folded leaves.

P. obtusifolia—An upright form with succulent stems and thick, waxy green leaves. 'Variegata' is a cultivar with green, milky green, and creamy white leaves. 'Gold Tip' has green and creamy yellow leaves. 'Minima' is a small-leafed green form.

P. rotundifolia ("nummularifolia")—A low creeper with thread-like vines covered with round, fat, waxy, pale green leaves.

Pereskia—see Cacti

Petrocosmea—see Gesneriads

Phalaenopsis—see Orchids

Philodendron

W, A, 1, M, E. Undoubtedly these are one of the best-known tropical American plants. The number of species is large; leaf size varies from small to very large, some are vines, and others form rosettes (self-heading). There are philodendrons for hanging baskets, bark slab training, trellis training, and even upright display. The durability and tolerance of these plants endears them to apartment dwellers. Propagation is easy from stem tip cuttings. A few of the many desirable species are described below:

P. andreanum—A beautiful climber with dark green, arrow-shaped leaves.

P. bipinnatifidum—This is a stout plant with a head of upright leaves, each split into 10 or 12 segments on each side of the midrib.

'Burgundy'—A good hybrid, this has green, arrow-shaped leaves with a reddish cast, red stems, and burgundy-colored young growth.

P. crenulatum—A self-heading form, this has deeply cut, curly-edged leaves.

'Emerald Queen'—Another hybrid, this has elongated, heart-shaped leaves and is ideal for totems.

P. hastatum—This is a lush climber with arrow-shaped leaves.

Philodendron ('Emerald Queen')

'Lynette'—This is a self-heading hybrid which forms a bird's nest-like rosette.

P. oxycardium ("cor-datum")—This is the old standby with heart-shaped leaves and vigorous vines. It is a tough plant which can be abused.

P. pertusum—This is actually the juvenile stage of *Monstera delici-osa* (see Mexican breadfruit).

Philodendron oxycardium

P. wendlandii—a self-heading variety, this forms a very attractive, moderate-sized rosette.

Phinaea—see Gesneriads

Phyllitis—see Ferns

Pick-a-back plant—see Piggy-back plant

Piggy-back plant, pick-a-back plant, mother of thousands *(Tolmiea menziesii)*

I, A, 1, M, E. A native of the western coast of the United States, this perennial herb makes an excellent house plant requiring a minimum of care. Its name derives from the development of young plantlets out of the bases of mature leaves. Leaves are lobed and toothed with a scattering of white bristles. *T. menziesii* makes a good pot or hanging basket plant. Propagate it from mature leaves that have attached plantlets.

Piggy-back plant

Pilea cadierei and other *Pilea* species—see Aluminum plant

Pilea 'Moon Valley'—see Moon Valley Plant

Pineapple—see Chapter 8

Pinguicula—see Meat-eating plants

Pitcher plant *(Billbergia)*

Pitcher plant

W, A, 4, B, D. Like *Aechmea,* this is a good bromeliad for beginners. Its flowers are more showy than *Aechmea,* but it is much less likely to produce colorful berries. Leaves are gray-banded, striped, or mottled; flowers are on long stalks and in pastel shades which contrast with the brilliant hues of the bracts. Propagation is by suckers or rootstock division in the spring.

Some good species for pots and hanging baskets are *B. amoena, B.* 'Fantasia,' *B. Zebrina, B.* 'Muriel Waterman,' *B. nutans* (Queen's tears), and *B. pyramidalis.* Most have contrasting rose or red bracts and blue flowers.

More information can be found under bromeliads in this chapter.

Pitcher plant—also see Meat-eating plants

Platycerium—see Ferns

Plectranthus—see Swedish ivy

Podocarpus macrophylla var. *angustifolia*—see Southern yew

Poinsettia—see *Euphorbia*

Polka-dot plant, Measle plant *(Hypoestes sanguinolenta)*

W, A, 2, M, E. This colorful plant from southern Africa has dark green leaves with a purplish cast and pink polka dots. As it is easily grown from seed and is quite unusual, it makes a good choice for raising house plants from seed. Children especially love raising this one. When growing, it is not a demanding plant; however, it needs severe pruning during winter to discourage the "leggy" look. Save the stem cuttings, as they propagate quite readily. It is best renewed yearly by cuttings, as it tends to get woody. 'Splash' is a good cultivar.

Polypodium—see Ferns

Ponderosa lemon—see Citrus

Pothos *(Scindapsus)*

W, A, 2, M, D. This southeast Asian plant resembles the philodendron in most ways, except that its heart-shaped leaves are lighter green and variegated in yellow, white, or silver, and its stems are somewhat square in shape. Pothos is a tolerant plant and will succeed in apartments where many other plants would perish. Like the philodendron, it can be trained to climb on bark. Propagate it by stem tip cuttings.

Pothos

S. aureus, which has waxy, dark green leaves with yellow variegation, and *S. pictus* which has waxy green leaves with greenish silver blotches, are two good species. 'Golden Pothos,' 'Silver Moon,' and 'Marble Queen' are good cultivars.

Powderpuff plant *(Calliandra inaequilatera)*

W, G, 1, B, E. If you want a tropical tree in a tub, this tropical Central and South American beauty is for you. It has feathery, graceful foliage and beautiful flowery puffs of red. A smaller grower is *C. emarginata* or pink powderpuff. Blooms may last six to eight weeks. If your house or plant room has a relatively high humidity, this is a moderately easy tree to grow.

Powderpuff plant

Prayer plant *(Maranta leuconeura kerchoveana)*

W, G, 1, M, E. Coming from Brazil, this low-growing plant has gray-green oval leaves with two rows of brown blotches which turn to dark green as the plant matures. At night the leaves fold upward, as if in prayer. In its native region the folding leaves channel dew to the plant. If your humidity is low, try this plant in a terrarium. More often than not, the foliage dries and withers in the fall. If this happens, cut the dry leaves off and water the plant once or twice a month until February, then resume normal watering. Your plant should revive. Another prayer plant, often called the red-veined prayer plant or nerve plant *(Maranta erythroneura)* is very attractive with its bright red veins. Propagate by division or leaf-

Prayer plant *(Maranta erythroneura)*

stalk cuttings. It is not too difficult to grow.

Princess pine—see *Crassula*

Pteris—see Ferns

Pussy ears *(Cyanotis somaliensis)*

I, A, 1, B, D. This is a succulent, little creeper from Somaliland. It is noted for its triangular leaves which are covered with white hair, hence its name. Flowers are purple and orange. Keep it shapely by pruning. It can be propagated by cuttings or by division. Of medium difficulty, it is a nice plant. Another species, *C. kewensis,* from Malibar, is known as the Teddy bear plant because of its brown, wooly hair.

Rabbit's foot fern—see Ferns

Rebutia—see Cacti

Rechsteineria

W, G, 2, M. D. These tropical South and Central American plants, which are members of the gesneriad family, have velvety green leaves and tubular flowers. The flowers are red, orange, or yellow. They do not present much difficulty to those who are able to grow African violets. Propagation is easiest from seed; tuber and leaf cuttings may present a bit more trouble. If you remove old stems, the dormancy period is very brief. Otherwise store them with scant watering in a dim, cool place during dormancy. There are low-growing and tall-growing species, but only the former are suitable for house plants. Of these, you might try *R. cardinalis, R. leucotricha* (Brazilian edelweiss), and *R. verticillata.*

Redbird cactus —see Devil's backbone

Red-veined prayer plant—see Prayer plant

Rhapis—see Palms

Rhipsalidopsis gaertneri—see Holiday cacti

Rhipsalis—see cacti

Rhoeo spathacea—see Moses-in-the-cradle

Rope hoya—see Wax plant

Rosary vine—see String of hearts

Rubber plant—see *Ficus*

Saintpaulia—see African violets

Sansevieria—see Snake plant

Sarracenia—see Meat-eating plants

Saxifraga sarmentosa—see Strawberry geranium

Scented geraniums—see Geraniums

Schlumbergera—see Holiday cacti

Scindapsus—see Pothos

Screw pine *(Pandanus)*

W, A, 1, M, D. From Malaysia, the Solomon Islands, and other nearby places, comes this old-fashioned plant. Since it is tolerant, it will adapt to most environments. Leaves are arching lances with sawtooth edges which are arranged in a spiral.

As it gets older, it gets large, sends out aerial roots, and drops its

lower leaves. Long before this occurs, it sends out suckers from which
you can start new plants to replace
that old, ungainly one.

The best one is probably *Pandanus veitchii* 'Compactus,' because
of its dwarfish nature and clear
green and white variegation. *P.
veitchii* and *P. pygmaeus* are also
good choices.

Sedum—see Stonecrop

Seemannia—see Gesneriads

Selaginella kraussiana—see Club moss

Selenicereus—see Cacti

Sensitive plant *(Mimosa pudica)*

W, G, 1, M, E. Native to Brazil, this spiny perennial has pinnate
feathery leaves. At the slightest
touch, the leaflets fold and close and
the stem droops. Easily grown from
seed, it can be kept as a house plant
for a year or two before its appearance becomes ungainly. My plants
put out an attractive puff of purplish
flowers. Children love this one.

Sentry palm—see Palms

Shrimp plant *(Beloperone guttata)*

I, A, 1, B, D. These Mexican
plants have wiry stems with oval,
hairy leaves. White flowers appear
at the ends of clusters of reddish
brown bracts on drooping spikes.
The flowers and bracts do resemble
shrimp. A cultivar, 'Yellow Queen,'
has yellow bracts. Plants tend to get
very "leggy" in the early spring;

Shrimp plant

prune them back severely when you put them outdoors in the summer. Propagate from cuttings of young shoots. These can be challenging plants.

Silk oak *(Grevillea robusta)*

I, A, 1; B, D. This Australian tree makes a carefree pot plant. It has silvery, downy shoots with feathery, fern-like green leaves. The silky hairs covering the leaves give them a grayish appearance. In California, silk oaks are often seen lining the streets. If you want a large, fast-growing plant, give this a try. It is easily propagated from seed.

Sinningia—see Gloxinia

Smithiantha—see Temple bells

Snake plant, Mother-in-law tongue *(Sansevieria)*

Snake plants

W, A, 1, M, D. This is an old-time favorite which is quite tolerant of adverse conditions and neglect. If you think you cannot grow anything in your hot, dry, dim apartment or house, you can grow *Sansevieria*.

Leaves are straplike, fleshy, pointed upright or ground-hugging rosettes. They are mottled or variegated in appearance. Sometimes clusters of dainty, white flowers will suddenly appear. *Sansevieria* are native to Africa.

Propagation is by division of the rootstock, which frequently sends up offsets on its own. It can also be propagated from leaf cuttings, if you keep the following two points in mind: One, make sure you know which end of the leaf cutting was nearest the base of the plant; roots only develop from that end, so it must be placed accordingly in the rooting material. Two, propagation of *S. trifasciata laurentii* by leaf cuttings results in the loss of the yellow strip around the leaf margin, so propagate it by rootstock division only.

Some interesting species are *S. parva* (upright, dark green on green leaves), *S. trifasciata* (upright, gray-white cross bands on green leaves), *S. trifasciata laurentii* (upright, yellow marginal leaf stripe), and *S. trifasciata* 'Hahnii' or Bird's nest plant (low ground-hugging rosette of leaves). There are many other species and varieties too.

Solanum pseudocapsicum—see Jerusalem cherry

Southern Yew *(Podocarpus marcrophylla var. angustifolia)*

C or I, A, 1, B, E. This is a semi-hardy evergreen that is grown outdoors in the South and as a pot plant in the North. Quite tolerant, it grows slowly and can add variety to your tropical foliage house plants. Keep it well pruned and use the cuttings for propagation. *P. macrophylla* 'Nagai' (from China) and *P. macrophylla* 'Maki' (from Japan) are two other good varieties.

Spathe flower *(Spathiphyllum)*

W, A, 1, M, S. This is a tough plant which can tolerate less than optimal light. It is a native of the Central and South American tropics. Leaves are lance-shaped, green, and glossy; sometimes white blossoms appear in the winter. Reduce waterings somewhat in the winter. Propagate by rootstock division. Two good species are *S. clevelandii* and *S. floribundum.*

Spathiphyllum—see Spathe flower

Spider plant *(Chlorophytum comosum* 'Vittatum'

Spider plant

I, A, 1, M, E. This is a dependable house plant that does well in most environments. It stores water in potato-like rootlets, so if you forget to water it, do not worry. When it matures, wiry stems emerge on which white blossoms appear. After they fade, young plantlets form and dangle from the stem, like "spiders." This species has white-striped narrow green leaves, forming a dispersed rosette. It comes from tropical Africa. Propagation is by rootstock division or rooting of plantlets. Another species, *C. capense ("elatum"),* has all green leaves and outgrows its pot more rapidly than the above species. They are both naturals for hanging baskets.

Staghorn fern—see Ferns

Stonecrop *(Sedum)*

I, A, 3, B, D. This genus of succulents has over 350 species spread over many countries. A wide diversity of forms can be found: blue or green leaves may be thick or needle-like; some species trail; others form rosettes or mats; and some are upright and bushy. They are all attractive and fairly carefree. Flowers can be pink, yellow, or white: They don't bloom too freely indoors, although they do in outdoor rock gardens. Propagate by leaf or stem cuttings, but allow them to form a callus for 24 hours prior to rooting. For additional information, see Succulents. Two of the many *Sedum* are described below:

Sedum dasyphyllum— This is a low-growing creeper-formingdense mats of blue-green. Leaves are opposite, tiny, and fleshy. It looks nice in small hanging baskets or as a ground cover in a pot.

sedum dasyphyllum

Sedum morganianum (Burro tail)—A beauty in hanging baskets, this has tassels of short, spindle-shaped leaves.

Strawberry begonia—see Strawberry geranium

Strawberry Geranium *(Saxifraga sarmentosa)*

C, G, 1, B, D. Also called strawberry begonia, this plant is actually neither a strawberry nor a begonia. It does, however, have runners like strawberry plants and leaves that are shaped like those of geraniums. It is not difficult to grow, providing it is kept in a cool location; it makes a good woodland terrarium plant. Native to China and Japan, it is a perennial herb

Strawberry geranium

which trails, making it ideal for a hanging basket or trailing over a pot rim. The bristly-haired, olive green leaves have silver gray near the veins and red undersides. Occasionally, white flowers appear. Propagate from the runners. A variety, *tricolor,* is also available with dark green and milky green leaves, marked with ivory white and red edging. It is harder to grow than the others.

Strelitzia reginae—see Bird of paradise

Streptocarpus—see Cape primrose

String of hearts *(Ceropegia woodii)*

I, A, 2, M, D. This plant from Natal, also called rosary vine, makes a good house plant, since it is not overly fussy. As a trailer, it looks unusual in a hanging basket with its thread-like stems set with pairs of succulent, heart-shaped leaves. The leaves are bluish in color with a silver marbling and purple undersides. Flowers are purple. Sometimes it shows signs of wanting to rest in the winter; if it does, decrease water. Tubers are produced in the soil and on the stems; they can be used for propagation.

Succulents

In general these plants are found in semi-arid and arid regions. They have fleshy leaves and/or stems. Nature has adapted them for our more arid areas by extremely reducing their body surfaces and thereby lowering their loss of water through transpiration. They have a natural capacity for water storage to help them survive periods of drought. Many assume unusual or bizarre shapes. Their root systems are usually shallow, enabling them to absorb any short-lasting surface moisture.

There are at least twenty families of plants which contain some succulents. One of the best known is the *Cactaceae* or Cactus family. Another is the *Crassulaceae* or Stonecrop family, which contains such species as *Crassula, Echeveria, Sedum, Kalanchoe,* and *Sempervivum.* The list of succulents is huge; no wonder some people specialize in them.

Most succulents are easily propagated from leaf or stem cuttings. Cuttings should be left in a dry place until the wound forms a callus. If they do not have one when they are planted, the chances are good that the cuttings will rot.

Many succulents make good, tolerant house plants. Cacti, holiday cacti, *Euphorbia,* living stones, devil's backbone, string of hearts, wax plant, *Echeveria, Sedum, Crassula, Kalanchoe, Haworthia,* and medicine plant are succulents that are discussed under their own headings in this chapter.

Swedish ivy *(Plectranthus)*

Swedish ivy

I, A, 1, M, E. This plant is not an ivy and does not come from Sweden. It is related to the coleus; some species derive from Australia and others from Africa. In general, leaves are rounded with sawtoothed edges; they have a waxy, shiny look. Flowers are pale whitish-blue. Some species are trailers and others are upright. Easily propagated from cuttings, this plant is relatively easy to grow. Since it is amenable to pruning, you can keep it shapely.

Probably the best and most common species is *P. australis,* which really looks great in hanging baskets. A variegated form, *P. australis variegatus,* has white patches and is also quite attractive. An upright species, *P. purpuratus,* has purple leaf undersides. *P. tomentosa* has "furry" leaves and is an upright species. *P. minima* is a nice trailer. *P. oertendahelii* has bright green leaves with silvery veins and purple edging.

Sweet olive *(Osmanthus fragrans)*

C or I, A, 1, B, E. This evergreen tree comes from China and Japan. Wiry twigs have holly-shaped, leathery, oval, green leaves with finely-toothed margins. Most notable are its small white flower clusters which are deliciously fragrant. Keep it pot-bound to induce flowering. It is one of the better tropical trees for growing in the house. Propagate it from summer cuttings.

Swiss cheese plant—see Mexican bread-fruit

Syngonium—see Nephthytis

Teddy bear plant—see Pussy ears

Temple bells *(Smithiantha)*

W, G, 2, M, E. These Central American tropical, upright plants are members of the gesneriad family. As such, they are no more difficult to grow than African violets. Leaves are heart-shaped and velvety green and are sometimes enhanced with red or bronze. Flowers look like nodding bells and appear on spikes from late summer into early fall; they come in shades of red, yellow, and pink. After blooming, the plants enter a dormant stage; during this time the soil should be kept barely moist. Propagation is achieved by division of dormant rhizomes or from cuttings of young shoots. Some excellent hybrids are 'Santa Barbara,' 'Abbey,' 'Carmel,' and 'Cathedral.' *Smithiantha* is often listed incorrectly as *Naegelia.*

Thanksgiving cactus—see Holiday cacti

Ti plant (*Cordyline terminalis* var. 'Ti')

W, G, 1, M, S. This plant is often confused with *Dracaena.* In fact, another name for this plant is common dracaena. However, it differs in that its leaves have petioles (leaf stalks), whereas dracaena leaves have none. A native of the South Pacific Islands, it is often used to make the grass skirts worn by hula dancers in Hawaii.

When mature, the Ti plant has a slender cane trunk with a spiraling rosette of arching, blade-shaped leaves. It is easily propagated by air layering, stem cuttings, or stem sections. In fact, stem sections capable of sprouting are sold in places like Florida (Ti log) or Hawaii (Hawaiian log). My own Ti plant was grown from such a log.

Ti plant

While this variety has green leaves, others have colored leaves. These include *C. terminalis* (copper green with red leaves), *C. terminalis* 'Firebrand' (purplish-red leaves, excellent house plant), *C. terminalis minima* 'Baby Ti' (small red leaves, good house plant), and *C. terminalis* 'Tricolor' (red, pink, cream over green, great house plant). In general *C. terminalis* and varieties succeed well in homes. There are other species of *Cordyline,* such as C. *baptistii* (green leaves striped with pink and yellow), which make good house plants. These usually grow best under conditions coded as W, A, 1, M, E.

Tillandsia

I, A, 4, M, D. These bromeliads make good house plants, but watch out because they can easily be overwatered. Leaves are usually narrow, long, thin and grayish green.

The best is probably *T. lindenii,* which has blue-purple flowers borne on spikes appearing from carmine red bracts. The popular Spanish moss, seen hanging from trees in the South, is in this genus *(T. usneoides).* See bromeliads for more information.

Tolmiea menziesii—see Piggy-back plant

Tradescantia—see Wandering Jew

Tree ivy *(Fatshedera lizei)*

C or I, A, 1, B, E. Sometimes called aralia ivy, this is a bigeneric hybrid between *Fatsia japonica* 'Moseri' and *Hedera helix hibernica* (Irish ivy). It is an evergreen shrub which can grow erect with support. It has five-lobed, leathery, waxy leaves of a lustrous green color. A fairly tolerant plant, it can adapt to less than ideal conditions. The same cannot be said of the variegated form, *F. lizei variegata,* which has creamy white leaf margins and is an attractive plant. Quite fussy, it needs less light (M) and water (D). Propagate all from cuttings.

Umbrella plant *(Cyperus alternifolius)*

I, A, 1, M, S. Related to papyrus, this clustering, perennial bog-plant comes from Madagascar. It has ribbed stalks crowned by an "umbrella" of bright green, grass-like leaves. Tiny green flowers do appear at times. Propagate by rooting the leaf crown or by division. As a house plant, it is quite easy to grow; it is even *hard* to overwater this one!

Umbrella plant

A dwarf variety, *C. alternifolius gracilis,* derives from Australia.

Umbrella tree *(Schefflera actinophylla)*

W, A, 1, B, D. This tree comes from Australia and is suited to tub culture. Leathery, glossy, green leaves form finger-like patterns which are arranged like "umbrellas" on the trunk. Not only is this a handsome, decorative plant, but it is tough. It is more correctly called *Brassaia actinophylla,* but has retained the above name in the United States. A smaller version, *B. actinophylla* var. *compacta,* is also available. Propagation is by air layering.

Velvet plant

Vegetables—see Chapter 8

Velvet plant *(Gynura aurantiaca)*

W, A, 1, B, E. As the name implies, the soft texture created by the purple hairs on the leaves gives a look of velvet. Bright sun is needed to fully develop the purple color. It is not too difficult to grow and requires pinching to develop a compact upright form. Propagation is easy through seeds or by cuttings.

Gynura 'Sarmentosa' is similar, except the leaves are scalloped and the plant has a twining characteristic; it looks great in a hanging basket. Flowers on both are small and orange. From personal experience I found the odor of the *G. 'Sarmentosa'* flowers is repulsive; I recommend you pinch off the flower buds.

Purple passion vine *(Gynura sarmentosa)*

Vriesia

I, A, 4, M, D. These bromeliads make stunning house plants.
They are very susceptible to water
damage, so be careful not to overwater them. *V. carinata* 'Marie' has
a yellow and red bloom and *V. splendens* (flaming sword) has outstanding black leaf stripes. See bromeliads for more information.

Wandering Jew *(Tradescantia, Zebrina)*—
Both *Tradescantia* and *Zebrina* are scientific names of this popular house plant.

Tradescantia—I, A, 1,
M, D. These plants
are native to Central
and South America,
although one species
is native to North
America. Trailers by
nature, they are ideal
for hanging baskets.
As house plants they
are good because they
are fairly tolerant. Leaves are
generally of a pointed oval
shape and flowers are usually
tiny and white. Propagation is
by stem tip cuttings. Species include: T. *albiflora* 'Albo-vit-
tata,' which has bluish green
leaves striped and edged in
white; T. *blossfeldiana,* which
has olive green leaves with purple undersides; T. *fluminensis,*
with bluish leaves and purple
undersides; and T. *virginiana*
'Alba,' an American native
with dark green leaves touched
with white wooly hairs.

Wandering Jew

Zebrina pendula—I, A, 1, M, E. These are trailing plants native to Mexico. Leaves are pointed ovals and usually striped. They make good hanging basket plants and are almost as carefree as *Tradescantia.* Propagation is by cuttings. *Z. pendula* has purplish green leaves with silver stripes. Varieties of this are *Z. pendula* 'Discolor' with coppery-green foliage overlaid and edged with metallic purple and splashes of red; *Z. pendula* 'Discolor multicolor' with greenish leaves striped and edged creamy pink and splashed with rusty red, silver, and purple; *Z. pendula* 'Minima,' a smaller version of *Z. pendula;* and *Z. pendula* 'Quadricolor,' a delicate plant with purplish brown leaves banded with white and striped with red and silver.

Watermelon pilea—see Aluminum plant

Wax begonias—see Begonias

Wax plant *(Hoya carnosa)*

I, A, 1, B, D. During our grandmothers' time, these plants were popular. The *Hoya* genus, which has many species and originated in southeast Asia and Australia, has varied leaf shapes. Leaves are leathery and glossy; some are varie-

Wax plant

gated. Flowers are waxy, fragrant, and colorful (white, pink, or yellow). The spurs on which flowers bloom reproduce flowers the following year, so do not remove the old flower stalks. Keep plants potbound for blooming. During the winter decrease water. *Hoya* are recommended house plants which look very nice in hanging baskets. They are easily propagated from cuttings.

Many species of *Hoya* are available. *H. carnosa* (which were the first house plant species), *H. australis, H. cinnamonifolia, H. motoskei,* and *H. keysii* are vigorous climbers suited to bark slab and trellis training. For variegated foliage try *H. carnosa variegata* (green, white, pink), *H. c. 'Exotica'* (two shades of green, yellow, creamy pink), and *H. purpureo fusca* (green leaves tinged with pink and flecked with silver). For unusual leaf shapes try *H. coronaria, H. carnosa compacta* (rope hoya), and *H. kerrii*. If your space is limited, try *H. bella, H. minima,* and *H. lacunosa.*

Weeping fig—see Ficus

Wood sorrel *(Oxalis)*

I, A, 1, B, D. These fairly common plants have clover-like leaves and dainty buttercup flowers in colors of white, pink, red, violet, and yellow. At night or on cloudy days leaves often fold and flowers shut. Some species have bulbs and others have rhizomes. Reasonably easy to grow, they are at home in regular pots or hanging baskets. For good yearly flowering, some species should be induced into dormancy after their blossoms cease and left to rest in a cool, dry place for three months. Propagation is by seeds, bulbs, rhizome division, and plant division. Some good species for house plants include *O. brasiliensis* (Brazil oxalis), after deep wine red flowers fade, induce into dormancy; *O. deppei* (rosette oxalis), give it a rest and enjoy brick red flowers; *O. lasiandra* (primose oxalis), crimson flowers; and *O. purpurea* (cape oxalis), white, rose, and violet flowers:

Woodwardia—see Ferns

Zebra plant *(Aphelandra)*

W, A, 2, M, E. These tropical Central and South American plants are noted for their gray-green or bright green leaves veined in white. Flowers and bracts appear as terminal clusters on spikes in the fall; they are long lasting. Keep these plants slightly

Zebra plant

pot-bound. After blooming is completed, prune them lightly and decrease the water slightly to give them a rest. They can be propagated from cuttings of partly ripened wood. With a minimum of effort this can be a rewarding plant. You might try *A. aurantiaca roezlii* (orange-red blooms), *A. chamissoniana* (yellow bracts), and *A. squarrosa louisae* (yellow bracts).

Zebrina—see Wandering Jew

Zingiber officinale—see Common ginger

Zygocactus truncatus—see Holiday cacti

Appendix

Additional Reading

While reading this book, your curiosity may have been aroused by some particular subject. If so, the following books, listed by subject may satisfy your needs.

African violets
> *African Violets, Gloxinias, and their Relatives,* by Harold E. Moore, Jr. New York: The Macmillan Co., 1957.
> *New Complete Book of African Violets,* by Helen Van Pelt Wilson. New York: M. Barrows & Co., Revised 1963.

Avocado
> *The Artful Avocado,* by John Canaday. New York: Doubleday Publishing Co., 1973.

Begonia
> *All About Begonias,* by Bernice Brilmayer. New York: Doubleday Publishing Co., 1960.
> *Begonias, Indoors and Out,* by Jack Kramer. New York: E. P. Dutton & Co., 1967.

Bonsai
> *Bonsai: Miniature Trees,* by Claude Chidamian. New York: Van Nostrand Reinhold Co., 1955.
> *Dwarf Potted Trees—The Bonsai of Japan* and
> *Bonsai: Special Techniques.* New York: Brooklyn Botanic Garden.

Bromeliads
> *Bromeliads, The Colorful House Plants,* by Jack Kramer. New York: Van Nostrand Reinhold Co., 1965.

Bulbs
> *Bulb Magic In Your Window,* by Ruth Marie Peters. New York: M. H. Barrows & Co., 1954.
> *Flowering Bulbs For Winter Windows,* by Marion C. Walker. New York: Van Nostrand Reinhold Co., 1965.

Cacti and Other Succulents
> *The Cactaceae,* by W. L. Britton and J. N. Rose. New York: Dover Publications, Inc., 1973. This was last published by the Carnegie Institution of Washington in 1937 and is now reprinted by Dover. It is a must for the very serious cacti enthusiast.
> *Cacti and Their Cultivation,* by Martin, Chapman, and Auger. New York: Winchester Press, 1972.
> *Cactus Guide,* by Ladislaus Cutak. New York: Van Nostrand Reinhold Co., 1956.
> *Handbook on Succulent Plants.* New York: Brooklyn Botanic Garden, 1970.
> *The Succulent Euphorbieae of Southern Africa,* by A. White, Dyer, and Sloane. Pasadena, California: Abbey Garden Press, 1941.

Ferns
> *Ferns and Palms for Interior Decoration,* by Jack Kramer. New York: Charles Scribner's Sons, 1972.

Flowering House Plants
> *Flowering House Plants,* by James Underwood Crockett. New York: Time-Life Books, 1971.

Fluorescent Light Gardening
> *Fluorescent Light Gardening,* by Elaine C. Cherry. New York: Van Nostrand Reinhold Co., 1965.
> *Gardening Indoors Under Lights,* by Frederick H. and Jacqueline Kranz. New York: Viking Press, 1957 (Revised 1971).
> *Lighting for Plant Growth,* by Elwood D. Bickford and Stuart Dunn. Kent, Ohio: Kent State University Press,

1972. This is for the serious fluorescent light gardener. *The Indoor Light Gardening Book,* by George A. Elbert. New York: Crown Publishers, Inc., 1973.

Foliage House Plants

Foliage House Plants, by James Underwood Crockett. New York: Time-Life Books, 1972.

Fruit Indoors

Dwarf Fruit Trees Indoors and Outdoors, by Robert E. Atkinson. New York: Van Nostrand Reinhold Co., 1972.
Growing Unusual Fruit, by Alan E. Simmons. New York: Walker & Co., 1972.

General House Plants

Exotica 3, by Alfred Byrd Graf. E. Rutherford, New Jersey: Roehrs Co., 1970. This is a pictorial and cultural encyclopedia guide to house plants for the advanced or serious house plant grower.
Growing Plants Indoors: A Garden in Your House, by Ernesta Drinker Ballard. New York: Barnes and Noble Books, 1971.
Making Things Grow: A Practical Guide For the Indoor Gardener, by Thalassa Cruso. New York: Alfred A. Knopf, Inc., 1969.
The New York Times Book of House Plants, by Joan Lee Faust. New York: Quandrangle Books, 1973.

Geraniums

All About Geraniums, by Peggie Schulz. New York: Doubleday Publishing Co., 1965.
The Joy of Geraniums, by Helen Van Pelt Wilson. New York: M. Barrows & Co., 1967.

Gesneriads

Gesneriads and How to Grow Them, edited by Peggie Schulz. Kansas City, Mo: Diversity Books, 1967.
Handbook on Gesneriads. New York: Brooklyn Botanic Garden, 1967.

Gloxinias

Gloxinias and How to Grow Them, by Peggie Schulz. New York: M. Barrows & Co., 1965.

Hanging Basket Plants
All About Vines and Hanging Plants, by Bernice Brilmayer.
New York: Doubleday Publishing Co., 1962.
Hanging Gardens, by Jack Kramer. New York: Charles
Scribner's Sons, 1973.

Miniature Plants
Miniature Plants for Home and Greenhouse, by Elvin Mc-
Donald. New York: Van Nostrand Reinhold Co., 1962.

Orchids
Growing Orchids at Your Window, by Jack Kramer. New
York: Van Nostrand Reinhold, Co., 1963.
Handbook on Orchids. New York: Brooklyn Botanic Gar-
den.

Propagation
Propagating House Plants, by Arno and Irene Nehrling,
Great Neck, N.Y.: Hearthside Press, 1971.

Terraria
Fun With Terrarium Gardening, by Virginie and George
A. Elbert. New York: Crown Publishers, Inc., 1973.
Gardens In Glass Containers, by Robert Baur. Great Neck,
N.Y.: Hearthside Press, 1970.

Variegated House Plants
Variegated Foliage Plants, by Paul Fischer. London: Bland-
ford Press, 1960.

Sources of Plants and Supplies

Once you have found a plant you like, or you need some
supplies, you will want to know where to find them. First try
the yellow pages or ask friends where they get theirs. There
is nothing better than to look at the item before you buy it.
However, there are items which may only be available from
mail-order suppliers. Some of these will be found in the following list. Many others will be discovered in the advertising
sections of garden magazines. Since there are many mail-order
firms, it is not possible to list all of them.

Many suppliers now charge for their catalogs. With the

present rate of inflation and the cost of paper and printing, it is an understandable practice. Some dealers refund the charge on your first order. As times change, so will the prices. Those given are subject to change, so it is usually wise to query first. If there is no charge, it is a common courtesy to submit a stamp.

The categories are not meant to be rigid. A place may specialize in one item, but still carry others. In time through experience you will develop your own mail-order listing.

PLANTS

African Violets
    Fischer Greenhouses
    Linwood, NJ 08221   20¢

    Green Thumb Home Nursery
    Ramsey, WV 25912   10¢

    Tinari Greenhouses
    2325 Valley Rd.
    Huntingdon Valley, Pa 19006   25¢

Begonias
    Logee's Greenhouses
    55 North St.
    Danielson, CT 06239 $1.00

Bonsai
    Allgrove Bonsai Farm & Nursery
    281 Woburn
    Wilmington, MA 01887

    Heirob Bonsai Nursery
    Toyo, Livingston Manor, NY 12758

    Hortica Gardens
    PO Box 308
    Placerville, CA 95667   25¢

Bromeliads
    Bennett's Bromelaids
    Box 1532
    Winter Park, FL 32789   first-class stamp

Cornelisons Bromeliads
225 San Bernardino
North Fort Myers, FL 33903   first-class stamp

Marz Bromeliads
10782 Citrus Dr.
Moorpark, CA 93021   2 first-class stamps

Bulbs
John Messelaar Bulb Co.
Rt 1 - A PO Box 269
Ipswich, MA 01938

P. De Jager & Sons Inc.
South Hamilton, MA 01982

Cacti and Other Succulents
Abbey Garden
Box 167
Reseda, CA 91335

Cactus Gem Nursery
PO Box 327
Aromas, CA 95004

Davis Cactus Garden
1522 Jefferson St.
Kerrville, TX 78028

Ed Storms
4223 Pershing
Ft. Worth, TX 76107

K & L Cactus Nursery
12712 Stockton Blvd.
Galt, CA 95632

Carnivorous Plants
Peter Pauls Nurseries
Darcy Rd.
Canandaigua, NY 14424   25¢

Plant Oddities
PO Box 127
Basking Ridge, NJ 07920

Ferns
> Edelweiss Gardens
> Box 66 H
> Robbinsville, NJ 08691   35¢

Foliage and Flowering House Plants

> Karutz Greenhouses
> 92 H Chestnut St.
> Wilmington, MA 01887   50¢

> McComb Greenhouses
> New Straitsville, OH 43766   35¢

> Merry Gardens
> Camden, ME 04843 $1.00

> Roehrs Exotic Nurseries
> R.F.D. 2 Box 144
> Farmingdale, NJ 07727

> The House Plant Corner
> Box 810
> Oxford, MD 21654   25¢

> Tropical Paradise Greenhouse
> 8825 West 79th St.
> Overland Park, KA 66104

Geraniums
> Carobil Farms
> Church Rd.
> Brunswick, ME 04011   35¢

> Cook's Geranium Nursery
> Lyons, KA 67554   25¢

Gesneriads
> Buell's Greenhouses
> Eastford, CT 06242 $1.00

Herbs
> Caprilands Herb Farm
> North Coventry, CT

> Rutland Herbs
> Box 583
> Georgetown, KY 40324 $1.00

Hoyas
    Loyce's Flowers
    Rt. 2
    Granbury, TX 76048   25¢

Orchids
    House of Orchids
    10 Bailey Ave.
    Oakland, NJ 07436

    Margaret Ilgenfritz
    Monroe, MI 48161 $1.00

    Rod McLellan Co.
    1455 El Camino Real
    South San Francisco, CA 94080 $1.00

Rare Plants
    John Brudy's Rare Plant House
    Box 84
    Cocoa Beach, FL 32931   50¢

    International Growers Exchange
    Box 397
    Farmington, MI 48024 $2.00

    Siskiyou Rare Plant Nursery
    522 Franquette St.
    Medford, OR 97501   50¢

Seeds & Nursery Stock
    George W. Park Seed Co.
    Greenwood, SC 29646

    Kelly Brothers Nurseries, Inc.
    Dansville, NY 14437

    La Vonne's Greenhouse
    463 2nd Ave.
    Riddle, OR 97469

    Peters & Wilson Nursery
    Millbrae, CA 94030 $1.00

    Stern's Nurseries
    Geneva, NY 14456

Sutton Seeds Ltd.
London Rd., Earley
Reading Berkshire R G61AB
England (From my own experience I suggest you
prepay for airmail delivery.)

W. Atlee Burpee Co.
Philadelphia, PA 19132

Terrarium Plants
Arthur Eames Allgrove
North Wilmington, MA 01887   50¢

Putney Nursery, Inc.
Putney, VT 05346

SUPPLIES

Fertilizers
A. H. Hoffman, Inc.
Landisville, PA 17538

Atlas Fish Emulsion Fertilizer
Menlo Park, CA 94025
(this is the common fish emulsion)

Charles Bateman, Ltd.
135 Highway 7 East
Thorn Hill, Ontario, Canada
(the more unusual fish emulsion that is rich in phosphorus and potassium)

United States Organic Ferto Corp.
PO Box 111
Spanish Fork, UT 84660

General Supplies
Bernard J. Greeson
3548 N. Cramer St.
Milwaukee, WI 53211

The House Plant Corner
Box 810
Oxford, MD 21654   25¢

Lighting Equipment
  Lifelite Inc.
  1025 Shary Circle
  Concord, CA 94520

  Shoplite Co.
  566J Franklin Ave.
  Nutley, NJ 07110   25¢

  Tube Craft, Inc.
  1311 W. 80th St.
  Cleveland, OH 44102

Terrariums
  Ambassador All Glass Aquariums, Inc.
  4403 Broadway
  Island Park, NY 11558

  Riekes Crisa Corp.
  1818 Leavenworth
  Omaha, NB 68102

  Visual Design Manufacturing Co.
  6335 Skyline Dr.
  Houston, TX 77027

Listing of Plant Societies

In the event your interests center on a particular group of plants, you may want to join a group of people who share similar interests. For the investment of a few dollars, you receive the group's magazine, answers to questions, plant and seed exchanges, and perhaps you will participate in shows.

No addresses are given below, since these are often subject to change when a new secretary is elected. Write to the following address for the current name and address of the secretary of the society of your choice.

The American Horticultural Society, Inc.
Mount Vernon, Virginia 22121

In Canada, write to:
The Director

Royal Botanical Gardens
Box 399
Hamilton, Ontario

In England write to:
The Secretary
The Royal Horticultural Society
Vincent Square
London, S. W. 1

Canada:
The African Violet Society of Canada
Cactus and Succulent Information Exchange

England:
The African Succulent Plant Society
The British Pelargonium and Geranium Society
The British Pteridological (Fern) Society
The Cactus and Succulent Society of Great Britain
The National Begonia Society
The National Cactus and Succulent Society
The Orchid Society of Great Britain
The Saintpaulia and Houseplant Society

United States:
The African Violet Society of America, Inc.
The American Begonia Society, Inc.
The American Bonsai Society
The American Fern Society
The American Geranium Society
The American Gesneria Society
The American Gloxinia and Gesneriad Society
The Bromeliad Society
The Cactus and Succulent Society of America
The Cymbidium Society of North America
The Epiphyllum Society of America
The Herb Society of America
The Indoor Light Gardening Society of America,
Inc.
The International Geranium Society
The Palm Society
Saintpaulia International

Index

An underlined page number after a plant name indicates a main reference to that plant.

259